Slowing

Slowing

Discover Wonder, Beauty,
and Creativity through
SLOW LIVING

RACHEL SCHWARTZMANN

CHRONICLE BOOKS
SAN FRANCISCO

Library of Congress Cataloging-in-Publication Data

Names: Schwartzmann, Rachel, author.
Title: Slowing : discover wonder, beauty, and creativity through slow living / Rachel Schwartzmann.
Description: First. | San Francisco, California : Chronicle Books, [2024]
Identifiers: LCCN 2024008970 | ISBN 9781797223759 (hardcover)
Subjects: LCSH: Time--Psychological aspects. | Quality of life. | Lifestyles. | Simplicity.
Classification: LCC BF637.T5 S44 2024 | DDC 158--dc23/ eng/20240318
LC record available at https://lccn.loc.gov/2024008970

Manufactured in China.

Design by Wynne Au-Yeung.
Typeset in Editorial New, Garamond Premier, and Neue Montreal.

10 9 8 7 6 5 4 3 2 1

Chronicle books and gifts are available at special quantity discounts to corporations, professional associations, literacy programs, and other organizations. For details and discount information, please contact our premiums department at corporatesales@chroniclebooks.com or at 1-800-759-0190.

Chronicle Books LLC
680 Second Street
San Francisco, California 94107
www.chroniclebooks.com

For my parents, who gave me my slow story—
and their enduring love and support.

End 162

Introduction

What more can I say about slowing down?

At first, I thought I was posing this question to you, but in reality, it's something I've been asking myself for years. A phrase like *slow down* is so often thrown around now: It's become a rallying cry fit for Instagram captions, a fleeting encouragement exchanged between strangers and confidantes alike. Slow down, and things will feel better—right? For me, the answer usually goes like this: better, occasionally—different, almost always.

In slowness, I've learned to differentiate between asking questions with genuine intention or purpose and asking them to fill space. But even before actively changing my relationship with pace, questions have always been integral to my life. *How does the sky feel close and far away at once? Isn't it funny that we like certain names? Do they seem afraid, or is it just me?* I didn't know it as a younger person, but I was building a practice of awareness even if, on the surface, my mind felt scattered.

At some point, modern life expected me to go fast and ask questions later, inevitably souring my curiosities. After spending nearly my entire adolescence and adulthood online, I realized that this change was partly a result of the digital age: It often redirects our questions and flattens moments, reducing our identities to the confines of a byline, job title, or social media post. Still, it's not all bad. I genuinely believe there is a more nuanced conversation to be had about living in a landscape that constantly competes for our attention.

In recent years, many of us have denounced hustle culture while trying to escape (and rebuild) the systems that make it so hard to see any other way to be. For that reason, slowing down is a practice, but it's also a choice. We must choose it every day. With that, I also choose to tell you the truth. The truth is that *Slowing* was born out of deep unhappiness—an unexpected beginning, a stressful middle, and an inevitable end—a story I yearned to revise. I no longer wanted my life's achievements to be predicated solely on validation and output, but I knew I still had something worthwhile to give—so I slowed my scroll, turned my back on those toxic notions, and began truly asking myself about time and pace.

Over the past few years, I've been writing my slow story in a new direction—away solely from career goals and external accolades toward something else entirely—but I haven't forgotten the moments in between. What you're about to read honors the details, questions, and choices that led to many other plot twists—the beginnings, middles, and endings that are part of my life and the lives of the people I've interviewed for this book. These life chapters laid the foundation for how I would structure *Slowing*. (After all, everyone's story—no matter how fast or slow—has at least one beginning, middle, and end.)

On the subject of beginnings: *Slowing* began as many different things: a collection of interviews, a more focused antidote to burnout. Form aside, I didn't believe I had enough to put myself on these pages, but as I dove in, I discovered I wanted to make room for things that weren't entirely new or profound but utterly ordinary. Because, in my decade-long quest for success, I lost that connection to my body and mind. I forgot how to breathe between asking the big (read: socially expected) questions. And in the exhale, I thought about everything that makes life enjoyable, tactile, and pleasurable. I considered what would happen if I slowed down enough to write about them.

I examined my pace through the lens of how I read, moved, dressed, showed up for people—or didn't—the list goes on. And while doing the actual work of writing, I started to live again. It wasn't easy: My anxiety became pronounced. I was forced to trust that I could share these darker sides in contrast to the sheen of my curated self. It was not so much an experience of "waking up"—I've been awake to the daily chaos that has cast a shadow over our lives—as it was a matter of accountability. I needed to understand time better and how I could intentionally proceed into new chapters. I needed to slow down enough to reclaim perspective. Writing this book saved my life because it reminded me that I have one—and an amazing one at that.

As an avid reader, I've grown to understand the intimacy that a book yields. To adopt that same care as a writer was a daunting task, though one wholeheartedly worth pursuing. Within these pages, you'll find fifty-two stories and meditations about time, pace, and creativity—mostly mine, along with original excerpts from my interviews with trailblazing creators—and a few supporting prompts throughout. Sink into one story each week or devour this book in one sitting; I leave the decision up to you. Though this isn't a self-help book, please help yourself to these sentences. Take these lessons with you to work. Rest your fingers on the spine. Tuck these secrets into bed with you. Let these slow stories humble you to the core, and—when you feel your feet beneath the ground again—finally exhale.

I've spent most of my life trying to establish some state of linearity, by putting one step in front of the other or checking proverbial boxes like you would on a to-do list. But *Slowing* reflects my truest experiences: Time and pace remain both energizing and elusive. Questions are asked and (sometimes) answered. Moments come full circle and seldom go in a straight line. Some stories are short and sweet—others are long and hard. The rest are still unfolding in real time. Because of that, there is so much beauty and truth here, too. And while I can't promise you'll find everything you're looking for, I hope reading these slow stories clarifies something about your own.

—RACHEL SCHWARTZMANN
January 2024

Beginning

DAWN

On Beginnings

Most of my stories begin in what is unseen—the fault lines: tiny flowers blooming from cracks in the sidewalk, the grout between shower tiles blanketed with late-night tears, a misty walk during a morning that'd rather be tucked away in Mother Nature's soft bed. For me, beginnings tend to take on the texture of spring. They are a fixed point in time, both beautiful and temperamental, buds yet to bloom on trees, reluctant storms that know they need to make way for clear skies. They are something to behold.

It was a late May morning when my dream of becoming a published author first came true. Within minutes, there was an expectation to celebrate. But I couldn't, not in the way I had been conditioned to, anyway. I physically couldn't raise my glass or infuse my voice with appropriate tones or inflections. It had little to do with my excitement or disbelief that a lifelong dream had come true—it was that I cared too deeply.

I cared to the point of paralysis. It startled me how haltingly this chapter in my life began, but I pressed on because I knew a deeper form of exhilaration was churning beneath the stillness.

Before this, I celebrated every milestone to show evidence of my gratitude. I prized excess and performance, indulging in beginnings without knowing how to tend to them after the mania passed. I didn't understand just how much energy it takes to care for something beyond the initial point of entry, how much of an intentional commitment it is to continue to work toward something after the initial fanfare has faded—because once the lights come up and the party ends, dawn creeps back around. We're left with the aftermath, though we can't disregard the mess. We have to kick the overflowing trash bags and deflated balloons out of the way and stumble back onto the path. We have to focus on what really matters.

As I've learned to cultivate a sustained effort of care, it's occurred to me to look at a beginning for what it could be: a slow start. The word *beginning* itself starts with *be*, and that is so desperately what I want: *to be.* I want to be awake to everything—the rainbow light trickling through the blinds in the warmer months and quietly fading as the year inches along, reconnecting with friends online and off, finding my feet on the floor again as a pile of laundry is (finally!) folded and put away.

I'm not saying there isn't room for gathering and cheers-ing and fun, but so often, beginnings are packaged as grand proclamations, actions, or revolutions. I've come to understand that a beginning is the most private moment we can

have. It's a feeling, a hope, a gift. A choice in how to greet the
world. When dawn rolls around, blink slowly and witness a
vibrant sunrise or cloudy heap. Easier said than done, I know.
Most days, I don't catch the bright pink sky illuminating the
neighborhood. I'm cocooned in darkness, hitting snooze
until life tells me I've overslept and missed out. Lying in bed,
my eyes still straining against sleep, I roll over and figure
now is as good a time as any to greet the day. I take my time
taking it all in.

But let me ask you something: Are you awake to it yet?
Your stretched-out legs dangling over the edge of the bed.
The cough caught in your throat. This new book in your
hopeful hands. The stranger—or strange phenomena—that
could upend your morning (or everything you thought was
true). No? Well, here it is—the beginning of everything:
a smattering of scents, words, and feelings to cast a shape
around your day. Start where you are, and then when you're
ready, turn the page. I have so much more to tell you.

Care and Be Aware

Awareness is a key component in building a solid foundation for care. Begin by cultivating awareness in all areas of your life. Consider the following prompts.

MONDAY: Define *awareness*. What does it mean to you in the context of your personal, professional, or creative life?

TUESDAY: Contemplate awareness. List the first words or ideas that come to mind when thinking about awareness.

WEDNESDAY: Question awareness. What are you self-aware of, and what are things you'd like to pay deeper attention to moving forward?

THURSDAY: Study awareness. Read books, stories, or media that engage in topics around awareness and care.

FRIDAY: Discuss awareness. Begin a conversation with trusted peers, friends, or family members about the role of awareness in your life.

SATURDAY: Practice awareness. Make space to observe or directly engage with the world around you. How has this week changed your understanding of this idea?

SUNDAY: Slow your awareness. Rest and read the next story.

MORNING
STORY

On Secrets

I sleep the deepest in the mornings, still lingering on the edge
of a dream. Shimmering light dances through the blinds in a
symmetrical pattern, eventually warming my bedroom and
rousing me back to consciousness. I can't always unravel the
previous night's imagery from what's actually real, but once
I'm able to keep my eyes open, outlines assume their full
form: the soft contours of my pillow, the chipped corners of
my black rubber phone case, my pilled socks and pale skin
tucked cozily inside.

The day begins. I move through the space, clumsily putting
my house—and myself—back in order. (Agenda: Make the
bed, try not to snag said socks on the jagged-edge floorboards,
drink some water, and struggle to form coherent sentences
until at least nine o'clock.) Once I've found a rhythm,
I remember to pay attention to things with less clearly

defined shapes: worries, ideas, and the like—amorphous but no less important.

Their presence is palpable as they take up residence in other ordinary objects. Worries attach themselves to mailbox keys, unlocking deep thought (and, on the best days, *hope*). Ideas propagate in houseplants; they luxuriate in the rich soil, growing from a seed into something worth pursuing. Goals balance on the edge of shiny batteries, charging devices, and the future. Secrets spread slowly in the blackened mirror of my freshly made coffee that's hot to the touch.

Yes, I said secrets. Let's talk about secrets.

It's funny to imagine secrets hiding in my morning coffee like little sugar cubes, delicious and—if not consumed in moderation—dangerous. Sometimes hard to swallow. When I bite my tongue or burn the roof of my mouth, I feel each secret falling through the space between hurting and healing—they're on their way back home, deep into my core. One small sip, and down they go.

When I was in my mid-twenties, I experienced a severe quarter-life crisis. More plainly put: I dreaded waking up. As sunlight cast harsh shadows across my bed, I kept my eyes closed, desperate to dream of another life instead of participating in the one I was already living—the one I had created for myself. My unwillingness to meet the day consumed me with guilt and shame.

I was a few years into building the style blog–turned–
content company I had initially started at eighteen years
old. I had planned on becoming a writer, but the digital
age presented an opportunity to take my love for storytelling in new, unexpected directions, so I let the path
unfold. A combination of hard work, resilience, luck,
and privilege alchemized into a circumstance that many
people are taught to yearn for: namely, being one's own
boss (it's something I'm grateful for but will continue
reassessing for the rest of my life).

Growing a business and growing up and growing into myself
against the backdrop of a volatile digital landscape (in New
York, no less) inevitably took its toll. Most of what I had
strived for, and achieved, was in direct opposition to my
solitary nature. Every morning, I wondered if this would be
the day I would admit that I could no longer work at the pace
I had been conditioned to believe was my baseline. That my
values were not in sync with the commercialized definitions
of success or happiness. That the insistence on performing
in a way that legitimized my position in these spaces left me
depleted rather than empowered. That my ambition was no
longer enough to see me through.

It took nearly three years for these concerns to materialize
into concrete action. So, as they festered, I continued going
through the motions: make coffee, keep moving. Sip after sip,
secrets became the most honest (albeit toxic) relationship
in my life.

○ ◑ ●

As a kid, I regarded secrets as a form of love. Whispering in a friend's ear, scribbling handwritten notes, and casting knowing looks at one another—all of those gestures meant something. Now secrets have come to represent a whole other level of intimacy, but they've also morphed into a form of currency.

During that period of tumult, I stored secrets away in what I likened to a savings account, whipping them out for necessary social transactions, rarely spending them on anything other than professional gain. Ironically, it was a time when I happened to be my most "outgoing." My calendar was often stacked with meetings, interviews, and events that were sold as a vital part of the millennial experience. Coffee dates were always favored.

My companions varied, ranging from fashionable clients and trusted collaborators to old friends. No matter the context, work orbited the discussion, and I demurred from saying too much as they asked things like: "What are you working on these days?" and "How's it going working with so and so?" and "What's next?"

Secrets can feel sacred in our culture of oversharing. Even when treated with reverence, they can be a lot to carry (especially when you don't know they are secrets in the first place). In many ways, I felt my secrets before I had the language to vocalize them. My feelings about what I feared or desired, I reasoned, were meant just for me. I often confused privacy with truths I didn't know how to confront: intuition I'd ignored, paralyzing doubt, and unavoidable change. Until I got my story "right," I figured it was better to be on the receiving end: nodding encouragingly and sipping my coffee as the people sitting across from me poured their hearts out.

Something big always seemed to be percolating on the tip of my tongue. For too long, secrets changed my taste buds. I adjusted to a palate of painful silence—the metallic taste of the unspoken in my mouth. I swished the words around and felt their hot edges melt against my teeth. I gulped noisily, sending the entire alphabet barreling down my throat. In my braver moments, I felt the soft outline of a *t* or *o* brush against my lips: my unfinished letter, written within, unsure of whether or not to come out.

I'm the friend that blushes at you even if we've known each other forever. It doesn't matter if you talk without pausing for air; I listen dutifully and chime in only after a few steady seconds of quiet have passed. When it's my turn to speak, I'm often asked to repeat myself, my voice quivering as I struggle to raise the volume. Over the years, my quietness has gotten clumped together with other descriptors: reserved, serious, gullible, boring, weak.

When I started to share my secrets, it was indirect at first. My uncertainty showed up in questions. *Why am I doing this again? Who am I doing it for?* My desire for change took up space in creativity. *I have an idea. Let me tell this story for you.* My fear emerged in pursed lips and sharp sighs. *I don't know; I'm not into it these days. I think I'm ready for a change.*

The work of our lives begins in the unknowing. We chart a path and do our best to stay the course. I've only recently realized that the duality of starting something just to tear it down later isn't something to be feared. It's what makes life interesting, humbling. But for a long time, I latched on to the notion that the beginning—of a company, a conversation, a relationship, a day—was unmovable. Once in motion, there was no room for subsequent error. In a culture that prides itself on loudness—signaling to the world that the higher the volume something is, the more it is worth listening to—the only way to use my voice was to feed the rallying cry deemed acceptable by the masses.

In my first life, the one before I knew how to draw clearer boundaries between work and self-worth, I longed for a sign of how to change my circumstances. Instead, I began to better understand the language of secrecy: Secrets, even when unspoken, didn't have to remain stagnant weights. Perhaps they were hidden opportunities. Perhaps they were new beginnings. Perhaps all I had to do was slow down, reach out, and finally speak up.

It was in the silken darkness of night when I closed the brand I had tethered myself to for nearly a decade. I sat on the floor, my bare legs warmed by a small, itchy rug, my elbows resting on the marble coffee table. My clock displayed a time that inched closer to dawn, and the heaviness of my eyes seemed to pull my entire body forward. The fluorescent laptop light beamed, and I could finally see where else my secret had been hiding: in sticky keys, my beat-up mouse. This accidental beginning fueled my desire to begin the next chapter of my story with intention. And with one final click, the website was closed. The secret was out—and over. (The book you're reading is what ultimately took its place.)

After working all night to move on from what had impacted most of my adult life, I was exhausted. Caffeine and caution ran through my body. I reached for my lukewarm cup of coffee, my fingers tiredly feeling for the mug's handle. When I looked down, I realized it was empty.

Secrets slow us down, offering time and space for private reflection and, when necessary, reckoning. While shapeless at first, they eventually transform into something pulsing and alive. In the liminal space between dreaming and living, I reached for the outlines of things, searching for distractions and grasping for something finite—I wasn't fully awake to the potential of what could change if I let go of the hidden parts of myself and made space for something new. This act is a release, an embrace, and an acceptance of a long-held belief: In the end, everything that's meant to reveal itself will.

So.

Let secrets hide in what you need and want most. Hold them in your car keys and let them ignite the way forward. Listen to them in your earbuds and let them replenish your creativity. Drop them into your coat pocket and let them pulse with possibility.

Let secrets inspire a practice of patience, connection, trust. Listen to your loved ones' slow stories—whether they're sad, happy, or scary—and when you're ready, tell them yours.

Let secrets scare you—just enough to wonder what happens if you never say your truth out loud. Because once your secrets are out, there is no telling where life will take you next.

Now, new secrets—not yet on the page—are growing into stories. Some of them will change a life. Parts of them will live on a screen. Others will remain right where they are, wrestling and writhing deep within. *Where to begin? When to share? When to let go?* I lift the coffee cup to my lips, priming my palate, deciding if this will be the morning I lay it all on the table.

Let(ter) Your Secrets Out

PROMPT

Secrets often hide in plain sight. As yours come into focus, let them out in the form of a letter. Complete the letter over the course of a week using these daily prompts—and remember: Just because you write it, doesn't mean you have to send it.

MONDAY: Begin by naming your secret. Who— or what—is it? How should it be addressed?

TUESDAY: Start your letter by setting the tone. Where are you writing from? What can you see in the room?

WEDNESDAY: Ask your secret a question.

THURSDAY: Tell your secret about how it would exist in or enjoy the world—and why it's time to let it out.

FRIDAY: Sign off with your hopes and intentions for your secret.

SATURDAY: After you've had some time away from the letter, think about the things you couldn't say or forgot to mention. Write these details in a short postscript.

SUNDAY: Rest and read the next story.

WAVE

On First Steps

I stood with friends in the middle of the street while their
one-year-old daughter Claire* found her footing. Just a few
weeks before, she had taken her first official step inside our
apartment, a small victory followed by a light plunk to the
ground. Even at this age, Claire wore her confidence and
questions proudly. It didn't surprise me that she was already
learning to move quickly.

The sky was dull, and the sun desperately wanted to set
behind a wall of gray clouds. A heat wave had gripped the
city that year, flattening color and sapping everyone of their
energy. Simultaneously exhausted and nourished from a full
day and dinner, we adults inched alongside Claire, who excitedly maneuvered over an uneven sidewalk in our Brooklyn
neighborhood. As we chatted, Claire continued waddling
but looked our way occasionally for reassurance, her wispy
blonde hair shimmering and as bright as her smile.

*Name has been changed.

When we reached a small garden bed, Claire's pace noticeably slowed. Shrieking with delight, she raised her limp wrist and suddenly began waving at what we realized was a pinwheel. The object was hard to miss, standing tall in a patch of dirt, surrounded by farm-animal figurines and a few tired plants. Its magenta, lime-green, and bright-yellow blades collided into one prismatic swirl, and as the wind picked up, Claire couldn't contain herself. "Oh, the simplest little things," her mom murmured.

Claire laughed and waved, and we laughed and waited. I watched her and wondered at what age we stopped seeing the world with our hearts.

○ ◑ ●

Everyone told me I'd cross a certain threshold once I turned thirty. That age (apparently) was a rite of passage. It marked the beginning of a decade that symbolized experience and maturity. Those first fumbling steps of adulthood would give way to hard-earned spotlights. Paying dues would become a thing of the past. Except that's not entirely true: As long as we pay attention, we continue paying our dues because there is always more to notice and, in turn, (im)prove. What changes the most—if we let them—are the goalposts around what we are proving and who we are proving ourselves to. That may be why I've become so taken with Claire's milestones.

Childhood is not without its hardships, but it's often rooted in the belief that we must try and keep trying, even if we take a step and make a wrong turn. There is nothing more impressive to me than someone who wanders happily without aim. *What if we allowed ourselves the same indirection as we aged? What if we acknowledged that there would be moments when we're lost in the margins, trying to find a new way back into our story?*

I've found myself increasingly resentful of societal timelines. I was the founder of a business at age twenty and changed direction close to thirty. Sometime in between, I began to call myself a writer. And as I've refined my craft, learning how to make it all mean something, I've grown to understand that first steps are a lot like first drafts: messy, indeterminate, and sometimes destined to fail.

Throughout our lives, creativity follows us around like a ghost. It heralds us when we're younger and haunts us when we're older. We scribble, draw, write—but no matter the medium, we've been conditioned to crave response. In an age of perfectionism, that response often comes from those who notice our missteps, which can leave us feeling bruised, reactive. But through time and experience, I've found a better way to make and move. I've recognized important first steps happen when we turn that reactivity into something intentional.

For those reasons, I've started to value *reciprocity* over *response*. The modern world has transformed response into technological value markers—response rate, response time—whereas reciprocity encourages attentive exchange. I am an only child with no child of my own. Despite this, the children in my life have reminded me there is no more illuminating exchange than one between someone at the start of life and someone starting over in their own.

As I watch Claire at the beginning of her story, I hope that one day her steps will transform into a confident stride. That she will wear her heart on her sleeve and that I will continue to roll up mine. But first, she will wave at the pinwheel, and I will commit words to paper, and together we'll stumble around the block and then into the rest of our lives.

Greet Your Firsts

PROMPT

We're often told not to dwell on the past, but recalling milestones or life-changing first steps can help us chart a path forward more purposefully. This week, take some time to greet your firsts.

MONDAY: Write about an important first step. This can be your earliest childhood memory or something more recent. What ideas or images come to mind?

TUESDAY: Write the first chapter of your story. Document the first things that come to mind, and don't stop until you've completed at least one page.

WEDNESDAY: Write about a first love. This can be about a person, place, or passion, or whatever feels appropriate. What words or sensations come to mind?

THURSDAY: Write about a first heartbreak. This can be in the context of love, career, creativity, or anything else. What colors or textures come to mind?

FRIDAY: Write about a memorable first change. How did this pivot unexpectedly impact your life?

SATURDAY: Write about a first adventure. This can be your earliest childhood memory or something more recent. What emotions or visuals come to mind?

SUNDAY: No writing today. Rest and read the next story.

FANNY SINGER

Writer and Founder of Permanent Collection

As told to Rachel Schwartzmann

Fanny Singer believes in infinite beginnings. The celebrated arts writer and cofounder of Permanent Collection gleaned this perspective from her mother, the revered chef and activist Alice Waters. As she embraces motherhood herself, Fanny is also recalibrating her relationship with pace. While Fanny is conscious of the inevitable shift that this life chapter will bring, she's not necessarily wedded to how things are. And if there's one thing Fanny wants her daughter to take away, it's that there is no manual for how to begin. "Beginnings can take very tortuous, twisty paths, and that's fine," she reflects during our call. "I would like to imagine that she feels confident in making her own path, which is horribly cliché, but honestly, I think it's going to be important in this world we inhabit."

"I think of myself as constantly engaged in beginnings. Everything is always, on some level, fresh to me. I don't think of myself as being in any seasoned or midpoint part of a career. I still feel like I'm at the beginning of many things, though I'm definitely at the end of other things.

To sit in that place of eternal beginnings is something I inherited from my mom. My mom is fifty years into having a restaurant, and she's still approaching it like it's a new enterprise—and all of the concerns that come along with it: her interest in sustainability, regenerative agriculture, education, and climate change. It's been an inspiration to me not to think of the work I do as finite or unchangeable. It feels subject to shifts—sometimes violent U-turns—and that sense of potential renewal keeps you interested in a given project.

Sometimes beginnings feel like they require contemplative solitude and, other times, the catalytic power of a conversation or collaboration with a friend. For instance, starting Permanent Collection—my line of design products—is something I would never have done if I hadn't formed a partnership with Mariah Nielson. So I do think some beginnings need another person involved who gives you the confidence, tools, or a complementary skill set to pursue something. But other things are more solitary. Much of the writing I do requires me to have a relationship with an artwork, an exhibition, or a place. That is individual. I think it varies.

There's a sort of beginning implied in the question: *What do we need to do now? What does the world need right now?* I've had the luxury of not necessarily having a life entirely revolving around politics. I've thought hard about very niche little corners of the art world. But increasingly, I feel a glaring urgency to have conversations that place our work and communities more centrally within the things that are existential threats. Not to be too dour or alarmist, but I find myself hungry to talk about what we can actually do. *What do we need? What can we do?* Those questions come up more and more. My friends are really engaged in politics, activism, and these questions. But it means that when we do gather, having these more provocative questions be part of the conversation is essential."

DRAFTS

On Creativity

I was freezing, then the cursor froze. The swirling rainbow popped up in its place, twirling for me, taunting me, as I tried to get words down before they vanished. It had been a grueling start to another winter, and I didn't know what I was still doing there, sitting at my computer, justifying the screen as a tool for my creativity. If anything, it felt more like a nuisance, but I had reached that point of no return—creativity and technology were one.

And at that moment, I wasn't sure I knew what creativity was to me anymore because it was seemingly everything and everywhere: a button, a prayer, an aesthetic, an accusation. What was once a part of my nature had become commodified and desensitized. Creativity lived in places I no longer wanted to touch.

These days, *relief* is the first word that comes to mind when I think about creativity. Finding myself beginning a project means there is a shape to it—even if I don't recognize it (*especially* if I don't recognize it). Writing a little every day helps. It's akin to waiting for the shower to warm up: You know you need to enter this space, and it'll take a moment to feel like something you can withstand.

Control comes after *relief* because there's never such a thing, and we always seem to want what we can't have. I'm often described as reserved and quiet, yet underneath the lilt in my voice is a longing for clarity so profound that it burns. My tongue burns. My cheeks burn. My heart burns. The words on the page burn because writing is a mirror that shows me everything. But I don't look away. I look and find a way.

I learned to look closely in one of my earliest creative lives. New York offered a way in when I wanted to become a professional dancer. One sweltering summer, I took a "Beginner-Intermediate" class at a beloved institution in the city, and I quickly discovered it was too advanced for me. I was undoubtedly a beginner in ballet, an intermediate in adolescence, rushing toward accomplishment in both. I crashed through the hour and a half alongside people obviously destined for the stage. That embarrassing beginning gave way to an important realization: I needed to look at myself and decide if it was worth it. I decided to keep going.

○ ◐ ●

Throughout my quest to understand creativity, I've learned to look in all directions and, by default, fall into step with distraction. It's a filter as much as a block: If something quickly takes my attention away, it's probably for a reason. The slowness happens when I meditate on the *how* versus the *what. How am I looking at or engaging with this? How am I spending my time? How am I approaching my work? How can I leave myself open to growth?* (I can never spell *efficiency*, so why prioritize it?)

In the intervening years of my dance practice, I valued studying more than performing. When I was accepted into a leading performing-arts high school, I couldn't believe my luck: I could take multiple dance classes every single day! I was an outlier in this regard. Unlike my classmates, I grew to dread the spring semester because that meant performance season was around the corner. Show after show, the movements I made were small and imprecise. The orchestra pit scared me. I was convinced I would fall into it, so it seemed impossible to willingly take up space on the stage.

Before I shed my first artistic skin, I learned how to live in it: I comforted myself after falling, sometimes literally, sometimes into confusion. I learned to move with callused toes in sticky canvas ballet slippers. I found alternative resources and designed my own summer intensives. I never took for granted the opportunity to train with storied choreographers. I became a person who knew creativity required tangible discipline and devotion. Though I couldn't escape the chilling fact that it would not be enough, and it would not be forever, it was somehow easy to overlook these premonitions. My creativity was still mine—very few people outside my inner circle were expecting much. Slipping out of success's clammy grip was still possible.

I'd grown fond of a teacher who taught an open ballet class on Saturday afternoons. She had a knack for maintaining the light in the studio even as the sun set outside. Despite the delightful ambience she imbued, I was always exhausted afterward—but it was the weekend, and I was young, so I still attempted to wander around the city after class.

As the sky faded to black and the wind chill registered, I felt the drip of my sweat-tinged skin go still and immediately sought shelter. I'd duck into a store, a coffee shop. I'd open books or playlists. I'd feel the adrenaline fading and something else setting in.

Much like the transition from barre to center (two components of a ballet class), I eventually learned to let myself pause before I was ready to go again. It was a relief to rest. Stillness was my control, if only for a moment. Only then could I muster the energy to appreciate that doing the work is worth it.

When I rest, I'm able to see creativity in the crevices. To recognize myself in Deborah Levy's elegant sentences. To sing along as Karen O screeches early-aughts hits in my ears. To feel calmed by the sight of Agnes Martin's subtle color palette. To contort my body into shapes demanded by Martha Graham's impossibly precise technique (though I don't do that much these days).

Practice doesn't always make perfect, but it makes something. If craft is practice, then maybe creativity is forgiveness— an acceptance (even warmth) toward a lack of finite output, an opportunity to not be too hard on yourself when nothing comes out. After all, there is effort, and that's all we can make: the effort to keep up during petit allegro combinations, to paint across a floor-to-ceiling canvas, to scribble illegible, meaningful words on a page, to scream until our throat screams in pain and our heart screams for us to stop kidding ourselves. But we can't stop—not really. We can only slow, which helps us see backward and eventually move forward.

Dance gave me a structure and a sense of camaraderie that sustained my creativity. Nowadays, I have to create more than the work itself. I have to create the time and agency. I have to create room to forgive myself for all the ways I haven't reached the finish line with flying colors. I have to believe in myself enough to let go. To try to make something with the courage, effort, and knowledge I've amassed. The instrument has changed since then—from my body to my mind.

I came back to writing in my mid-twenties as a means of coming back to myself. But even with the wealth of creative inspiration and my own experiences, there are days when I'm still trying to figure out what writing is supposed to do other than take my hand off the phone and across the page. Then as words materialize, I realize it joins me to something real— and now you're here reading it, so I guess it joins me to you, too. It's a comforting thought because, as I said, I was freezing as I sat at the beginning of another winter. I was no longer a beginner in life. I had everything to do and nothing to lose—so I opened this document. The cursor finally unfroze. The wind picked up, and time exhaled. I shivered in anticipation. I felt a draft, then I wrote one down.

Create a (Conscious) Plan

PROMPT

It's possible to create with intuition and intention—but planning can help actualize your artistic goals. Consider these daily exercises as you create a (conscious) plan.

MONDAY: Begin by doing nothing. When a new idea or goal comes to mind, wait until the initial urgency passes. If it sticks around, then you'll know it's worth pursuing.

TUESDAY: Share your idea with trusted confidants. Discuss themes, hopes, or worries and see what comes back. What do you hope to make or achieve?

WEDNESDAY: Put pen to paper and begin drafting your vision or idea. What tangible steps must you take to get things off the ground?

THURSDAY: Write about creativity and forgiveness. How does the relationship between the two affect your current outlook?

FRIDAY: Engage in what brings you joy (without attachment to output). How do you feel while pursuing these activities? Think about how you can integrate this mood or approach into your creative practice.

SATURDAY: Spend a day outside with nothing to distract you from the elements. When you get home, list colors, symbols, or textures you noticed from the natural world, and reference this list when you need additional inspiration.

SUNDAY: The best-laid plans require rest. Rest and read the next story.

EVAN LIAN

Cartoonist

As told to Rachel Schwartzmann

Childhood daydreaming helped Evan Lian fulfill his artistic goals. Instead of using his school planner to take notes, Evan would fill its pages with drawings. When Evan went on to study accounting and finance, his creativity slowly resurfaced after finding himself back in a familiar environment. "I was studying for an exam for a professional license in the banking industry and found myself drawing again in the margins of my notes," he says. Something clicked for Evan. He set his sights on working with the *New Yorker*, where he landed his first art acceptance in 2018. Today, Evan's process is less regimented, with a renewed emphasis on play and exploration. Still, he remains careful with his art as he understands the fraught nature of beginning a project in the digital landscape—one often synonymous with performance and external validation.

"Beginnings are just opportunities; maybe we hold them a little too precious. Something that I've found in both my day job and cartooning career is that—especially with barriers to entry a bit lower than they have been in the past and because of technology—we can start things almost as frequently as we want. I find what holds people back from beginning new things is wanting them to be perfect or starting with a certain amount of success, followers, or traction. Realistically, you have an opportunity to start any creative endeavor or enterprise whenever you want. Usually, the biggest hurdle is your own reservation.

It's easy to get complacent or get into routines. Beginnings are a way to shake up your understanding and push yourself to grow continually. I think there is value in being uncertain or uncomfortable because that's when you have the most opportunity to learn. Cartooning is my primary creative practice, but I often find that if I burn myself out, I reach for other things. Beginning something is like a pressure release, expressing yourself in different ways and keeping that creative muscle going.

I think more people should ask: *Why not?* Most of the time, the risk you face is looking slightly naive. People think there are a lot of reputational risks in the social media environment. There is a little bit of that, where people try to put on their best front, or they want to present the best version of themselves or feel they have to monetize their creative practices somehow. I would push back against that and say: Why can't we just do things—make art, start something—just for the sake of trying something new?

Who am I? I'm just a guy who started drawing cartoons at his desk! Part of what drives me is that I want people to have that same realization: Whether or not you can make a living off of it doesn't matter. You can make creatively rewarding things. You can have creativity be a part of your daily routine without necessarily having to change your LinkedIn bio. You can just start."

RUSH
HOUR

On Routine

Rush hour changed when I moved to New York City. Car-pooling and sleepy suburban roads were now a thing of the past. At just twelve years old, I was afforded a rare opportunity to assert my independence. I howled with friends as we rammed into disgruntled adults on the city's congested streets. I "surfed" on the subway, showing off my balance as the train swerved through tunnels. I people-watched but hadn't yet learned how to see their stories.

The ritual of rush hour became entwined with societal performance as I grew older. Having a clear destination indicated a sense of stability and success. It said something worthwhile about me, often quieting the voice within: *You are not good enough. You don't deserve to be here. Go this way instead.* My mind felt rattled, but my movements were marked by purpose.

Like many things in modern life, commuting is an imperfect process: Passenger discourse can derail your entire mood; schedules are almost guaranteed to go awry. It's a test of endurance and attention. At each subway station, I collected my belongings—and bearings—as people flew by. I observed (and at times empathized with) my fellow riders' urgency, though I hoped their commitment to a quickened pace was motivated by enthusiasm just as much as obligation. After a time, I began to question whether commitment and enthusiasm were mutually exclusive. As soon as I turned that question inward, everything stopped.

The inclination to build a routine is akin to fulfilling a wish many of us have: establishing a sense of security. But throughout my early twenties, I had a much narrower view of routines and rituals, often looking to the commercial wellness industry for solutions. I recognized the appeal of reaching for something soothing in times of distress. At the same time, what was marketed as a routine worth having wasn't always sustainable.

During the pandemic, and as isolation became the norm, my outlook on routines changed. We collectively sought understanding and connection. We pulled on the masks and built (virtual) bridges. My now-husband suggested we re-create rush hour to add structure to the day. "Let's get up and get a coffee," he would suggest wearily. "Let's do a loop at lunch and again after dinner." With each of our quarantine walks came a painful reminder: We had rushed by one another for so long. It had taken global crises to remind us that a routine we'd grown to resent became something we'd have to reimagine or, at the very least, not take for granted.

I began to see things through a shifting lens: from fast to slow, solo to shared, routine to (simply *being*) en route. Rush hour, I realized, could be about so much more than a single destination or mode of transportation. Commuting could be an exercise in community. Because however lost or aimless we feel—no matter what we are doing or where we are going—we all share the universal experience of moving through the world.

There's comfort in enduring the unknown alongside people who are shaping the pages of our stories in ways we never expected. Slow down, and you'll see what I mean: a polite smile from a stranger as you enter your favorite coffee shop, animated conversation from passersby, rapturous laughter of teenagers as they convene at the crosswalk. In these moments, humanity eclipses fear. Doubt gives way to hope. Our routes may be different, but together we are heading somewhere.

It had been two years—too long—since I entered the station. I nervously rocked back and forth on my heels as the F train rumbled toward the platform. The doors screeched open, and clusters of people—some clad in masks, others enveloped in headphones or cradling sleepy infants—stood and slumped and sat in all corners of the train car. I squinted to make out any available space, gradually realizing that I no longer fit in the way I once had. I was twenty-nine and felt decades removed from the person who once viewed rush hour as a gateway to the future. A familiar inkling of dissatisfaction crept in. I watched people shove their way through, barely making out the last echoey instruction to stand clear of the closing doors. While the train pulled away, I watched my reflection blur against its steel body.

○ ◑ ●

I no longer have a clear route or routine. When I do find myself aboard, I'm more observant, peering through the shadows that once conveniently hid unwelcome truths. I'm also infinitely conscious of the space around me: what I take up and how much I give.

I've always positioned myself near the train doors, with my back facing the window. It's a tight spot but it remains the quickest escape, even if I don't always know what's waiting on the other side. But how much can we ever really know about what's beyond our vantage point? This unpredictability makes it easier to change my mind about how I move through the world like I used to change trains. I can turn around, even if it causes a slight delay. I may end up somewhere entirely new. I can begin again. More often than not, I have to.

Even now, the city's crowds remain steadfast, rarely dispersing. Sometimes, when it feels like too much, I retreat—to the middle of the platform, sidewalk, park—and watch people go about their day. They have somewhere to be. And when I'm ready to join them, I take a deep breath and a step forward, remembering I'm a part of this ecosystem—this life. Slowly, one foot in front of the other, hour after hour. The only thing I rush toward is possibility.

○ ◑ ●

Redefine Your Rush Hour

PROMPT

When can urgency become intention? Reconsider—and redefine—your rush hour by incorporating these prompts into your daily routine(s).

MONDAY: Write down where you want or need to go and how you plan to get there. Are there ways you can slow down while en route? How can you make more time to notice the little things?

TUESDAY: Create a playlist that calms you during busy periods.

WEDNESDAY: Show a small act of kindness to a loved one or stranger during your rush-hour commute.

THURSDAY: Queue up the latest podcast or try a different snack. Add something unexpected to your rush-hour routine.

FRIDAY: Take note of a scene or person that moves you while you're moving. What about this moment inspires you?

SATURDAY: Redefine your rush hour. Take stock of these experiences, and write an updated definition more aligned with your values.

SUNDAY: Don't rush today. Rest and read the next story.

ALLISON STRICKLAND

Artist

As told to Rachel Schwartzmann

From painting to dressing up and spending time out-doors, Allison's childhood was ripe with artistic explora-tion. These early awakenings informed her professional path in the performing arts. But after experiencing burn-out, Allison returned to visual art, culminating in the start of her ethereal meditation painting series. This particular body of work feels nourishing to both Allison's commu-nity and individual practice—and the arrival of the digital age has enabled her to share these works far and wide. As Allison navigates this landscape, she contends that, medium aside, she is first and foremost an artist.

"Endings and beginnings are intrinsically linked for me. I'm at a point in my life where all my beginnings are standing on the shoulders of endings. So I would define a 'beginning' as the reset, the inhale, the breath of fresh air: Everything that I was doing or that I was before is done. Sometimes beginnings feel like they're clearly asking, *What am I going toward?* But a lot of times, what I'm going toward is really informed by what I've left behind. The challenging part is to let things end when they want to and not when I want them to. Now my beginnings feel faster and braver because I'm not so afraid to lose things anymore.

Many times beginnings are: *I'm going to step into the unknown*—at least, that's been my experience. That's definitely how my meditation painting started. It was truly from my own need of wanting to do something that brings me peace and makes me feel at ease. I would've never thought that creating these small meditations in my sketchbook would have ended in any work, much less large-scale work.

I'm very slow to move because I like to understand *why* I'm moving. I've been that way since I was a kid—if I don't understand why I'm doing something, I have a tough time doing it. Then once I understand why, I tend to be very impulsive and impatient: I understand it now; why is it not fully manifested?! So my lot in life is finding the balance of these two things: *Where can I be a little faster than I'm comfortable? What am I waiting for? And where can I tease out the patience?* The hardest part about that is relinquishing control around it. I think it's allowing myself to be present and realizing that slowness isn't a long game. To me, it's being very in the moment. You can only be slow right now.

You cannot only inhale; you have to exhale, too. There are times when you have to research and do absolutely nothing. We're not meant to create constantly. Entropy is part of the creative process, not a hindrance to it. People think if it's not all at once, it feels like failure. There is this pressure—we are so goal oriented as a society—and that's where you can slip into the journey conversation. It always feels corny to say, 'Oh, it's not the destination,' because the destination also feels amazing when you get there, but I think there is an element of: *What does the process of success feel like?* Success is not necessarily a crescendo—it's a practice."

TIMESTAMPS

On Attention

00:00 For every love story, there is a sad story.

1:00 For every broken heart, a million tiny ones pop up in its place—in our lives, on our feeds.

2:00 But when a heart shows what we like (and who likes us back) and then quickly disappears, we're just as eager to chase it back into existence with the same urgency.

3:00 If we can't find it, our hearts break. Our attention shatters like a million shards of broken glass.

4:00 As we dislodge these tiny crystalline reminders from our mind's eye, we don't realize the scars are already forming everywhere else.

5:00 It's so easy to look away from the truths they'll tell us—so instead, I keep looking at my phone, scrolling until I've forgotten what brought me there in the first place.

6:00 There are moments when I truly want to throw my phone out the window.

7:00 Because if left to my own devices, I'll let *this* device throw me into a swirl of distraction and love, which I tend to mistake for the same thing.

8:00 I can't catch my breath, but I still catch your eye.

9:00 Once, I wrote an essay about writing *to* notice rather than to *be* noticed. The irony is that the piece was noticed far and wide.

10:00 And then I noticed how much I've been writing/worrying/thinking about how our relationship with pace translates online.

11:00 But we're often taught or conditioned to believe slowness is supposed to *look* a certain way.

12:00 What "style" does slowness wear these days?

13:00 What language does it speak?

14:00 What would it mean to forsake what we love for aesthetic or thematic continuity?

15:00 (In other words, should I stop posting my sweaters?)

16:00 What are we not seeing—liking, *learning*—when we're focused on satisfying the wrong heart?

17:00 Who are we when we're performing our values rather than living them as humans?

18:00 Will these questions inspire you to slow your scroll? For a moment, maybe.

19:00 This story began in a digital tug-of-war. The prize? My attention. Yours, too.

20:00 But I've learned there's so much we don't see even when everything is at our fingertips.

21:00 For every love story, there is a sad story. A slow story.

22:00 For every digital heart, a million real ones beat loudly— in our chests, under our sweaters, and around the world— if we remember to pay attention.

23:00 By the time this book is in your hands, I hope I've made my case.

Pay Attention to Your Intention

What would happen if you made art for no one's attention but your own? Consider your relationship with creative attention by answering the following prompts.

MONDAY: What motivates you to create—the process or the product?

TUESDAY: What's more exciting to you—creating or sharing?

WEDNESDAY: What matters more to you—the how or the why?

THURSDAY: What feels the most natural to you—quiet or conversation?

FRIDAY: What encourages you—seeing or being seen?

SATURDAY: What endures in your practice—attention or intention?

SUNDAY: Rest and read the next story.

VIRGINIA SIN

Founder of SIN

As told to Rachel Schwartzmann

Virginia Sin has always had an entrepreneurial spirit. As a child, she ran a make-believe grocery stand and found solace in art, but despite this recurring thread, Virginia wasn't necessarily encouraged to pursue a creative career. "It was a very typical immigrant family upbringing," she recalls during our conversation. "I'm Chinese American, and to my parents, design and art were not a way of making a living." After a short stint studying economics in college, Virginia transferred to art school and later moved to New York to pursue a job in advertising. There, Virginia slowly found herself on the brink of a new beginning with a time-honored medium: ceramics. "I missed the tactile projects I had in school. It was a big transition to move from California, and I needed a creative outlet. I enrolled in a ceramic class, and it's actually where my first product was born." Ultimately, Virginia's talent and determination translated into her namesake brand, SIN.

"The beginning of something can often be a spark at first—a flash of lightning. You have a thought that runs through your mind and exits quickly; you don't really think about it again until maybe the next time it happens. When something keeps coming back into my mind, I grab it and realize it needs a little attention. That is, to me, the beginning: whether it's a business idea, a story I want to tell, or a product I want to design. It's important to acknowledge that there isn't a black-and-white start time. It can be multiple events that happen and accumulate to become more official.

I love the idea of constantly becoming better at whatever you do or want to become. I often like to think a lot about past experiences, in which, given another chance, I maybe would've navigated something differently. The questions I want to ask before a beginning are: *Have I done something similar to this before? What was that outcome? How can I do it differently to start a beginning in which I have more control of the narrative?* I enjoy challenging and pushing myself in that way. The downside is that maybe I'm a bit hard on myself because I'm always thinking about how I could have done something better. I end up having to remind myself to live in the celebrations and acknowledge the successes so that I'm not so focused on creating better versions of new beginnings.

I'm very reactive—so I've learned, when making important decisions, not to reply to that email, sign that lease, or get back to that person until I've sat in (what I call) discomfort. I don't love waiting, but often, thoughts will pop up during that window. The more I do it, the more comfortable I become operating that way. I'm seeing the benefits of slowing down.

When it comes to creating a product made in clay—all of it is timing. This is a good metaphor for life: *When do you join these two pieces together? At what state? What's the moisture level?* If one part is drier than the other, it will not adhere. If you rush a slab and join it, it's going to collapse. Ceramics teaches you patience. It forces you to be more mindful of the time and the appropriate time for a specific process.

We can practice being mindful and listening to what our bodies tell us every time we have that urge to make a quick decision or to react. It doesn't mean that you should turn off gut instincts—you can still listen to them—but taking a beat or two to acknowledge that moment will get us really far. Slowing down is all relative: minutes, hours, days. I haven't mastered being mindful at all, by the way. It's something that I am constantly working on. It's challenging, but I try to practice it—the more I do, the better I hopefully become at it."

WINTER

On Style

I once wrote that winter is a whisper: You feel its sharp breath on your ear, and as quickly as the feeling registers, it vanishes. For me, it's a period when words don't always flow as freely— where stripped branches catch them midsentence, hardening their edges, and they sit like buds, waiting to blossom into something worth saying aloud.

As winter stretches across an ending and a beginning, I'm unsure of how to orient myself in time. But somehow, each year, I fashion myself into someone who knows a thing or two about the world. I can count on clothes to do the talking. I look ahead and create a look to live in. While matters of aesthetics can seem trivial, reclaiming simple functions like getting dressed offers new ways of thinking about everyday magic.

In winter, everything is laid bare—and we take cover from life's questions, both big and small. We layer on top of our vulnerability and reticence. We style our discomforts and learn to pay closer attention to details that help us piece ourselves together or meet ourselves again. In my case, when January tips over like a rollercoaster halted at its pinnacle, I see each week in shades of blue: ice earrings, cobalt coats, and navy beanies. February comes to me in romantic hues: soft sweaters of ballet pink, gentle lavender, and buttery yellow. March tells me to proceed slowly, its light-green eyes glistening with mischief as I struggle to dress to its constantly changing command.

Slowly, winter's palette begins to pill like my favorite sweaters. Time slows down as gray blankets the ground and sky. There is some visual reprieve, though: I watch others' pink noses scrunch as flushed cheeks soften and red tongues unravel colorful stories. Language keeps them warm in a season that otherwise calls for silence. And when I can't find the words to match theirs, I can almost always find hints of meaning in my closet. I sift through ornate accessories and oversized wool turtlenecks and remember that, more than anything else, I'm dressed in life experience. I'm ready to try on another year. I'll grow into its mishaps and mysteries. I'll tailor my dreams so that they fit more snugly. I'll wonder what to ask the world and what it will ask of me. But first, I'll wrap these precious months around me like a well-worn coat as I brave whatever comes next.

Style Your Story

PROMPT

Sartorial play can help us renegotiate what everyday magic looks like in our life and style. Consider integrating "style" into your life with this week's prompts.

MONDAY: Describe your relationship with style. Write about how it (positively) shows up for you personally, professionally, creatively, or sartorially.

TUESDAY: Dress in "life experience." Wear a garment or accessory that symbolizes your growth or a past chapter. Write about how wearing this item makes you feel.

WEDNESDAY: Reflect on your muses or icons. Write about why they exude "style" and what elements of their work, aesthetic, or mission ignite you creatively.

THURSDAY: Style your space. Photograph the objects, artifacts, or mementos that add meaning and beauty to your environment.

FRIDAY: Style the seasons. Write about how you approach style each season and how weather, mood, and temperature impact your process.

SATURDAY: Style your story. Write about the pieces, words, or ideas you would like to try on at this point in your life.

SUNDAY: Wear your best off-duty clothes. Rest and read the next story.

SOPHIA ROE

Chef, Writer, TV Host

As told to Rachel Schwartzmann

Sophia Roe has a lot on her plate, but she's never too busy to begin again. The celebrated chef, writer, and television host feels the most attentive in the kitchen. When it comes to pace, Sophia is quick to admit that she's constantly navigating the tension of working within spaces that require long-term commitment— like food justice and agriculture—and consciously listening to other perspectives. "We're going to have to come together," she says. "That's the part of my job that requires slow ease, mindful joy, and kindness. That's the part that I do have to manage and keep really slow. The urgency is the topic. The urgency is hunger. But the slowing down and being methodical is when you really get into the nitty-gritty. You start getting into the systems. It's a really interesting balance for sure."

"A beginning is the kindest, sweetest, simplest thing. The beginning of any moment that happens matters to me. Those are the things that I think about all the time. Even when I walk away from someone I've never met before, it's my first time with this person, and that's not an ending. It's just the beginning. Who knows when I'll see them again? And I also think about what an impact that person's had on my present. What an incredible thing that has completely changed the nature of my day. I think communities are only communities if you actually attempt a connection—even if it's just a wave or a smile.

I'd love to go as slow as molasses if I could. It doesn't feel like that is something people find value in anymore. The older I get, the more I love that something is just going to take the time it takes. Everybody asks: 'Soph, when are you coming out with a cookbook?' I don't know, whenever it writes itself! Good sentences are hard to come by. Good sentences said at the right time are even more challenging to come by. Good sentences said at the right time and heard by the right people— that's almost impossible. I just don't work best when I'm rushed.

It's very important for us all to feel entitled to forget about anything we want and completely start over. I think that's what's most pressing of all. So much of life is about your past informing your present and your past informing your future. I want everybody to understand that a beginning can have nothing to do with where you came from. It can have absolutely nothing to do with what you've been through. It can just be as organic as a thought. That is the coolest thing in the world. We should all feel entitled to forget things that don't feel good, that weren't good for us, and that hurt us.

I'm definitely a woman entitled to forget and know exactly what it is to start over. I have such a great relationship with starting over because I know I absolutely deserve to. I deserve a new apartment, a new beginning, a new relationship, a new friend, or a new outfit. A new anything—a new skill, a new teacher. So many people have anxiety about starting new things or attempting to start new things based on the past. *What if I mess it up? What if it ends up like the last one? What if that other thing happens again?* I feel like so much of our past informs our beginnings, and I don't think it has to be that way if you don't want it to be."

LINES

On Reading

For many years I didn't open a book. I was new to adulthood and distracted by everything. The lines that gripped me were not on a page. They were weaving outside of gritty music halls and overpriced cocktail bars, inside echoey sample-sale venues and packed airport terminals. (Real estate was a story I bought into so quickly at that point.) While I came away from this period with new experiences, these places—and the lifestyles attached to them—put strenuous demands on my time, which made it difficult to read consistently. It wasn't until I reached my mid-twenties that I understood how much of an unexpected (and accidentally self-imposed) barrier to growth was created in my life.

But this wasn't always the case. Elementary school first confirmed my love of stories. (Standouts included *Amelia's Notebook*, *Harriet the Spy*, *Little Women*, and the *American Girl* series.) During silent reading—as books came out of cubbies and a rare calm descended upon the room—I also learned how to read people. When I found my attention drifting from the text, I let my eyes rest on my classmates. I observed the small, dimpled lines on their faces metabolize stories from past decades or ones conceived from thin air. I saw true natures emerge in those quiet moments: when sweaty hands gripped tattered classics and nothing but the sound of annoyed sighs and No. 2 pencils tapping loose-leaf paper pierced the air.

As I got older, my peers taught me there were other ways of reading—and telling—the truth. Class presentations presented an opportunity for empathy: There were teary explanations of haphazard family trees, show-and-tell about objects that symbolized a marriage before its undoing. My turn always came around like a song on repeat, and it never got easier. I hated standing at the front of the room, reading aloud to a half-listening audience. I felt detached from the content, but as my voice quivered, I assigned new meaning to the task: I faced my fear.

And if we're talking about fear, I think it's worth mentioning that I always feared getting in trouble. On the rare occasion that I did, I realized the powers that be were afraid I'd finally figured it out: I could rewrite the rules. A shy girl could make a loud statement. A young person didn't have to follow a prescribed path, especially based on others' perceptions or expectations. Love and grief could be endured and processed at any age. Rules looked different than boundaries.

I had long been rewarded for being amenable, but when high school ended, so did my patience. Reading had become a gateway to finding myself. Then a new life chapter tumbled off the paper and into my lap—I was growing up, and there were other things to do—I picked it up and ran.

After a period of running ragged, I managed to slow down. Reading felt different by then. I wasn't sure how to turn to the page, because, for so long, I had cast books off as a way to experience living with little commitment—after all, I could slam a book shut at any given moment. Real life couldn't be so easily opened and then abandoned. Nor should it be.

By thirty, I had grown both personally and professionally. I got married. I was hyperaware of everything and everyone. For a while, paying such close attention to things exhausted me—but as I stepped into a new chapter of adulthood, I understood that storytelling was more than an action, or a trend, or a personality trait, or a hobby. It was essential in a world that often lacked empathy. Each time I finished a book, signs of my awareness blanketed the ground like seeds. I couldn't unknow any of the sentences that shook me awake—like Ross Gay's elegant asides or Durga Chew-Bose's astute meandering. I would never truly forget what I learned from them: that words can change life just as much as they can affirm it.

Now, I read to change and be changed. To understand how to live between the lines. To absorb what is said in the silence. To meet people without ever hearing their voices. To get real. To slow down. To grieve what I know deep down will never be. I read to reacquaint myself with a world whose constantly shifting realities unhinge us from certainty, expectation, and each other. I read and ask myself: *Where should these stories*

transport us? How long should we stay there? When do we
give those precious words back? And to whom do they belong?
Do they bring us back home, or do we build a new home made
of their question and exclamation marks?

I might have found the edge of an answer to these questions
on a cold winter night when my husband's leg brushed against
mine. The spines of our books touched as we sat cross-legged
on the floor with our rabbit sprawled out beside us. There was
no classroom or distraction. It was silent, and we were reading.
He read fact, and I read fiction. The pages reminded me of
something true. If I kept paying close enough attention, the
lines formed a path back to a story I know well but will never
truly finish: my own.

Read between the Lines

PROMPT

What is the role of storytelling in your life? Read between the lines and consider how words and language shape your life by incorporating these prompts into your week.

MONDAY: Read and write. Read your standard texts—books, media, or whatever content you usually like to consume. Write about how they're affecting your life.

TUESDAY: Read and reread. Read your favorite short text. Then at the end of the day, reread it. Write about what's different upon the second read and how this time or setting has impacted your mood.

WEDNESDAY: Read and question. Pose a question to a character in your favorite book. Write their imagined answer based on what you know about them rather than what you'd like them to say.

THURSDAY: Read and listen. Try reading with ambient noise in the background. Write down the words or phrases that remain in focus amid the distraction.

FRIDAY: Read and emphasize. Read the people in your life and talk to them about their current personal, professional, or creative chapter. Write an imagined scenario about life in their shoes.

SATURDAY: Read and move. Read billboards, posters, or other camouflaged texts outside your home. Write a list, short story, or poem with phrases that stuck out from those messages.

SUNDAY: Read (the next story) and rest.

LAST
NIGHT

On Time

As a child, I had long mermaid hair and an even longer memory, though both were often tangled. For a while, I could only measure time in nights—specifically *last* night. "Last night," I would begin in my stretchy, little-girl voice before launching into a detailed retelling of an event that might have happened yesterday or a year ago. It didn't matter. It was clear in my mind, so I said it with my heart.

Even as I learned to tell time, I struggled with the mechanics of it. I felt out of my element when seconds bloomed into minutes. Once, my class sat in a circle on the floor and watched the small clock on our classroom wall tick forward, and my teacher asked: "What time will it be at a quarter past two?"

My hand shot up almost instantly. "Two forty-five," I blurted with rare confidence.

The teacher looked at me hesitantly and shook her head. The kids around me snickered, and one boy cut in with the correct answer. "Two *fifteen*," he said with such emphasis that it felt like an attack.

This is my last concrete memory of *learning* time: getting it wrong. It's funny to place *learning* and *time* next to one another (given that we supposedly learn more about ourselves as life progresses), but I often misunderstand them. One lesson has stuck with me, though: Time has a way of showing us our mistakes. Whether we learn from them is another story.

Here is something that I've learned about myself in recent years: I don't necessarily want to tell time to slow down. Instead, I'd rather tell time to stop altogether—even if it's just once. How would time interject if I tried to tell it that I wanted to vacation in the past without the reminder to live in the present? That I wanted to be suspended in my most intense moments of happiness, sadness, and fear and watch myself in hindsight? Time may blink slowly at first, a small smile spreading across its face, and then rage with reality: You can tell time all you want, but it answers to no one.

I'm quick to use the word *regret* when thinking or talking about the past. But I don't want that to be the case. So, with the time I have left in this life, I'll find a gentler and more forgiving word. *Revel?* No, too flowery. How about *reckon?* No, not everything requires such force. Maybe it's simpler than I think. Perhaps the word I'm looking for is so widely used when discussing what makes us whole that we forget to remember it. Yes: *remember.* My word is *remember*—I don't regret last night; I *remember* it, which is to say, I remember that what I've experienced, said, wondered have all unfolded under the same sun and sky regardless of age, circumstance, and place. Last night is every night and day. It's winning and losing and growing. It's everything, and it matters.

Last night, I was an infant, and that only lasted for a little while.

Last night, I went to sleep in one state and woke up in another.

Last night, my most enduring friend and I fell out, and six years went by in silence.

Last night, I accepted that I would never hear from her again.

Last night, I danced at Lincoln Center and realized this was not the only type of performance I would give.

Last night, I wondered if it was bad that I could see the veins in my face and head, and the internet told me not to worry (too much).

Last night, I went to a party at a cabin in Queens, got drunk enough to take my shoes off, walked barefoot in the rain until my car picked me up, and then walked away from a scene that was never mine to begin with.

Last night, I walked forty blocks through Manhattan with a boy I loved but would never be with because he was learning how to be with himself.

Last night, I *walked* in the bike lane because, contrary to what they say, you *can* forget how to ride a bike and also forget how to get where you need to go.

Last night, a family member I no longer spoke to passed away, and my heart exploded with guilt because I was still too mad to say goodbye.

Last night, I forgave and then forgot why I was mad for so long.

Last night, the world shut down, and I stood on my stoop at 7 p.m. to join the chorus of clapping and cheering for the doctors and their hard work.

Last night, I built a résumé instead of a life.

Last night, I realized that anything could change.

Last night, I thought about the little girl who couldn't tell time. She told stories instead.

Tell Time What You Want

PROMPT

What would happen if you suddenly told time who you were and what you wanted? How would you feel? Consider your relationship with time by incorporating these prompts into your week.

MONDAY: Tell time who you are and how you've changed since childhood.

TUESDAY: Tell time what you need and who you miss.

WEDNESDAY: Tell time about a season in your life that was good.

THURSDAY: Tell time a story from your past that you can't tell anyone else.

FRIDAY: Tell time what or where you'd like to begin again.

SATURDAY: Tell time an answer to a question you'd like to be asked more often.

SUNDAY: Tell time that you're going to read the next story and rest.

REMEMBER THE GOOD

On Home

I haven't seen my mother in three years. Our parting is hard to describe, so I'll begin with this: Seeds were planted, and roots took shape. The wind picked up, I grew up, and we grew apart.

When I was a young person, change was the constant. But my parents and I learned to feel at home in our forest of ambiguity. I sat against the tallest tree in sight—my mother—shaded under a leafy canopy of maternal protection. It appeared sturdy, though I didn't yet understand that bad weather could bring everything down in one swift motion.

At first, I found these figurative storms thrilling: They signaled that I was in the world—becoming more aware of its functions and promises—even as they pervaded my family's life. Ultimately, the sights grew less scenic, and I was unable to recover as quickly from each parental blowout or pivot. What I had presumed to be steadfast took on a different form.

The landscape morphed from dynamic into something less stable. I slowly rose and backed away, fearing the weight of it would come bearing down.

○ ◑ ●

The San Francisco flat is a place I only know through photographs and home videos. There I am, wrapped in a towel, fleshy baby rolls—read: croissant legs—peeking out from the edges. There's me again, taking my first wobbling steps down the carpeted hallway. And again, running butt naked, squealing with delight. My mother captured everything with care.

The house in Vallejo was newly built. Dust bunnies and metallic bugs lived and died in its empty corners. On move-in day, I slept on the floor in a pink sleeping bag while my mother waited for the last moving truck to arrive. As she likes to tell it, a massive tarantula emerged seemingly out of nowhere and beelined in my direction. Her strength would waver in the following years. But that day, she saved me from an eight-legged beast.

The house in Lodi had a classic California orange tree. Shaded by its leaves, we'd sit and watch our dwarf rabbit hop around the front yard. Eventually, he would hide in the bushes along the side of the house. My mother, on her hands and knees, giggled in frustration. His fur blended in with the earth, making it hard to distinguish where he began and ended. It could take hours to coax him out. But there was laughter here, even when they found my mother's tumor.

The next Lodi house was large and imposing. It was haunted in more ways than one. We had recovered from health battles and an attempted family separation. My mother and I felt ghosts breezing by us on the rickety stairs.

The big, red-brick "mansion" in the small Texas town made *us* the ghosts. We knew that the South could never be our forever home, especially after the company that brought us there laid my father off. This home housed our mounting sadness. My parents' violent words seeped into the carpet, tinged with the scent of alcohol and stained with tears.

The apartment in Forest Hills was a second chance. It became our crash pad when we weren't in the hospital visiting my mother. My father worked nights, and I immersed myself in all New York had to offer a burgeoning teenager. At home, my mother stood on the balcony railing, sneaking a cigarette. I got sick here, too, and was out of school for months. My mother struggled to help me regain solid ground. She placed our faithful Maltese mutt on my pillow while I napped. She led me outside for daily walks.

The houses in Rego Park were our final attempts to make a home together. My mother got hurt at her office and eventually stopped working. Our family fractured irreparably. In the first house, our cairn terrier escaped through the fence, squeezing through the bars and taking off toward Queens Boulevard. My mother tried to chase him, clad in pajamas, me following behind, the Maltese mutt trailing us all. My mother's cries rang throughout the streets. She couldn't catch him.

In the second Rego Park house, my father moved into the basement, leaving my mother to putter around the remaining floors. She couldn't catch him. Soon, she couldn't catch me.

The apartment in Astoria broke my mother and me after things shattered between her and my father. Her health challenges worsened, and dozens of pill bottles rattled in kitchen drawers. The television droned at all hours of the night. Her loneliness took a seat at our table, joined by fleeting romances that blossomed into one particularly tumultuous relationship. The man that appeared in our kitchen one day after school, shirtless, cooking lunch for my mother, lingered. His presence made my withdrawal more pronounced.

I've lived at more than a dozen addresses across three states. Many of these residences marked a pivotal chapter in the story of my mother and me. It's only now, situated in a home of my own, that I've been able to think more critically about the places that defined our relationship. As I've gained miles and life experience, it's become harder to ignore pressing questions: *How do we make a home—or return home? What do we owe one another? How—or when—do we move forward?*

It's hard to unpack a lifetime's worth of mother-daughter intricacies, so all I can say is that I slowly began to equate my mother's love with her pain—a condition that plagued her for too long. But her expectations of me remained the same: I was her daughter. I was to accept her unconditionally. It was a test I would fail again and again.

While mistakes were made on my mother's end, too, her youthful wonder remained, buoying her to become the perfect parent to a young girl. Together we relished fairy-tales, tea parties, shopping trips to the mall, and late-night talks about love. Even as a child, I could feel how much she prided herself on being my mother. She lived and breathed it. Her role steadied me even as our environments changed. But life began tearing through the seams of her curated appearance. I couldn't find her as she shape-shifted from the mother I knew as a girl to the woman who no longer knew herself. Change had been our constant for so long; our private battles widened the gap between us. Even so, she tried to be there for me as best she could.

As adults, we've made a home in the digital space. My phone log remains sparse, but my mother takes up the most real estate there. The thick red font indicating missed calls matches her urgent tone. A text notification pops up. It remains unanswered until an emotional tug-of-war ensues. Dozens of paragraphs arrive out of order. Missed calls give way to frantic voicemails: *Just calling to check in. I'd like to touch base. I don't understand this silence. Please let me know if you got this.* I ignore them all, defending my decision to let us both calm down, knowing there is a hint of defiance and control on my end. My mother's plea remains consistent in these disparate exchanges: *Please, remember the good.*

For years, my mother has been trying to break through to me, invoking a tone I haven't responded to since I was a child. The daughter she raised has transformed into some-one reserved and distant. I often steel myself against her, my voice monotone, treating her advances as an affront rather than an invitation. Every question she asks feels like a trap. Too much time has passed; I no longer know how to answer when she calls.

○ ◑ ●

The last time I saw my mother in person was difficult. Her health problems persisted, relegating many of her days to shuffling between doctors' offices and her ground-floor apartment. The space was either cozy or drab, depending on your mood. When John and I arrived, I tensed at her forced cheeriness. We sat quietly together, me on the edge of the chocolate-brown chair, John on the white leather couch with my mother at the other end. We balanced Hanukkah-themed paper plates on our laps, inhaling the awkward silences. Even with my partner present, she grew tired of my resistance and ordered me to my former bedroom as if I were a petulant teenager. I felt an emotional storm brewing.

The air in my room was stale, and the light was faint. A few antique figurines lined the shelf above my old desk. My mother stood firmly in front of the door, holding the knob so I couldn't leave. Then, she took a shaky, deep breath. "Why don't you like me?" she asked, tears streaming down her face.

What kind of a question was that? What was I expected to say? But the fear in her eyes rocked me so deeply I could only look away. She waited for my response as I gazed at her cane resting on the wall behind us. I thought about how we'd had to heal alone, our hearts breaking and our bodies hurting in new and old places. For so long, I'd held on to the past like a weapon that could be reloaded. I saw my mother. I lived with my mother. I loved my mother. But I didn't know my mother, and she didn't know me—not really. I hadn't allowed her to. What would happen if I did?

I wanted to tell her that *like* was the wrong word. I wanted to trust my mother. I wanted to trust myself.

"I do like you," I whispered, meeting her foggy gaze. We stood in silence until she nodded and stepped away from the door.

○ ◑ ●

I couldn't shake the image of the old bedroom shelf from my mind. Its sparse decoration reminded me of what used to reside there: journals bookended by odds and ends. Not long after the incident with my mother, I flipped through one of these teenage relics, a fat pink journal whose cover proclaimed, "Keep Calm and Eat a Cupcake."

I stumbled upon an entry dated April 18, 2011, 2:53 p.m. I was a few weeks away from graduating high school, and "Memories" was the only thing I'd written. The word preceded a series of photographs of my mother and me from my childhood taped on subsequent pages—

In color: My mother wears a red blouse, blue jeans, and dark lipstick. Her arms are around me as we perch on a zebra, rising and falling on the Golden Gate Park carousel. I'm looking away. She's smiling.

Black-and-white: My mother holds me in her arms, pointing to something in the distance. I'm looking away. She's smiling.

Black-and-white: A portrait of us together. Our heads are touching, forming the shape of a heart. My lips are parted, tiny buckteeth hanging from the roof of my mouth. My hand rests on my mother's cheek. I'm looking away. My mother looks directly at the camera, her eyes bright. She's smiling.

Black-and-white: My mother and I are on the tire swing at Golden Gate Park. We're sitting across from one another, looking at the camera. Both of us are smiling.

We are in the world in these photographs—locales outside the walls that often confined us.

We are in the world in these moments—but we also feel at home with each other.

My mother now lives in Northern California with her best friend. She tells me that she no longer feels connected to the West Coast and wants to return to New York—where I still live and where we first ruptured—but I've started to remember the moments in between. I've learned that remembrance sits somewhere between attention and acceptance. It's a reckoning that brings us closer to truths that were so easy to disregard when our hearts were pulled in a million different directions.

Remembrance is life between deep breaths. Had I been able to remember the small moments between the familial milestones, I may have recognized my mother's life—and strength—sooner. I may have also been able to accept how different we are as people, though that does not cancel out our love for one another.

My mother might still be searching for her home. But by remembering every detail that makes her whole, I realized I could make a home for her *here*, in the pages of our slow and enduring story.

It was an overcast afternoon when I got engaged in the woods. The sky was pale, a palette somewhere between languor and hope. John and I embraced under the lush trees surrounding our cabin. We called our parents one by one, elated and teary as we shared the news. When I brought up my mother's number, I bit my lip. It had been weeks since we'd spoken by phone, but in the few texts we'd exchanged, her tone had been lighter, indicating gradual improvements. She had driven for the first time in over a decade. She was taking considerable steps to renew her professional life. Her communication was clearer, and her questions felt less pointed. I was happy for her. I was surprised by my happiness. I was saddened by my surprise.

When I called her, it didn't take long for her to catch that what I had to say was big—sharing something with genuine enthusiasm felt foreign to me. After a few excited squeals (and obligatory questions about the ring), she paused and said, "Well, I guess there's no denying now that you're all grown up."

I was a few months away from turning thirty, but I humored her anyway. "I guess not," I said, laughing.

I tried to conjure an image of what she looked like at that moment: her river-blue eyes, layers of vintage jewelry, and timid smile. Those were things that remained consistent against the backdrop of so much turmoil. Perhaps she was cuddling her dog or gazing at the vanity in her room. I'll never know for sure. Instead, I concentrated on what I knew to be true: behind me, a forest thrumming with life; next to me, the man I love; and within me, an acceptance that my mother and I would never fully move in the same direction. Still, I wondered if we'd finally found common ground or, at the very least, a new foundation.

We leave home behind but find it again in the people we love and who love us. We weather the unknown; it wears us down and builds us anew. Seeds are planted, and roots take shape. Sometimes we emerge as something unrecognizable, but we grow just the same. Like each season sweeping through the world, my mother—with her sunrays and her storms—always comes back. In her wake: expansion and wreckage, rebuilding and change. It's a cycle as old as time.

I haven't seen my mother in years. When I see her next, I know she will stand in front of my door and look at me with love. This time, I will open it a little wider. I will remember the good.

Remember the Good

PROMPT

As you reflect on important chapters in your story, try to remember positive details or moments when you felt most at home.

MONDAY: Where do you feel most at home? Write about or discuss this location with a trusted confidant.

TUESDAY: What moments have made you smile? Write a list of phrases or words that call a positive memory to mind.

WEDNESDAY: Walk down memory lane. Go on a walk and call a friend or family member. Reminisce about a time or place that meant a lot to you both.

THURSDAY: What has *good* meant to you in the context of your life so far, and what does it mean now? Write a new definition.

FRIDAY: Remember a good deed that was done for you—and then pay it forward with an act of service like a donation or kind note.

SATURDAY: Capture the good. The next time you're experiencing a blissful moment, document it: in a photo, piece of writing, or sketch. Set a reminder to look back at what you've created one year from now.

SUNDAY: Rest and read the next story.

Middle

DAYLIGHT

On Crossroads

The clocks remain unchanged when daylight savings arrives.
The oven timer stays at 2 p.m. while my phone tells me it's
1 p.m. I'm outside of time in these moments, which makes it
hard to know what to do next. It also doesn't help that I have
a habit of falling into habits: Patterns emerge, and I become
accustomed to sameness, comforted by an unchanging day
even as hairs go gray and wrinkles take up residence around
my eyes. In an age where we're conditioned to crave newness,
I struggle to justify to others why I've enjoyed pumping the
brakes to virtually zero.

I'm writing to you from a place of discomfort—retreat.
If you haven't seen me for dinner dates or birthday parties,
or for months as they stretch into new seasons, I'm sorry.
I've fallen out of touch with wonder and, by default, the
world. I've been fighting with someone I love about why
what we already have can't be enough: a roof over our heads,

shelves filled with books, food on the table. (Such gifts!)
Although monotonous, things have felt manageable for the
first time in a long while—so why rock the boat? How can
I give up this sense of safety, especially now?

As days stretch out a little longer and sunlight beckons me
closer to the window and then finally onto the street, I recognize that I might have conflated pace and possibility. After all,
that's what living is: rocking the boat. What other alternative
is there? Float until the weight of withheld desire, longing,
or inaction topples us overboard?

I'm no longer sinking, though I'm not yet swimming.
I'm drifting at a crossroads: a place with the clearest edges
that hurt when life's waves pummel me toward them,
a place that forces my hand to make a decision, a place
that forces me to see beyond the tide.

I now know that it's enough to slow down and even settle
down, but I shouldn't settle for less: experience, discovery,
truth. I'm remaining open while maintaining a semblance
of normalcy. I'm in the middle of a day in which the sun will
set past 7 p.m. for the first time in months. I forgot what
it means to feel the light just as much as see it. I forgot to
change the clocks, but they remind me it's okay to look back
and move forward—and I will, eventually.

Sketch What Scares You

PROMPT

We sometimes must face old fears in order to decide where to go next. Consider the following exercises as you create a new path forward.

MONDAY: Sketch something or someone you were scared of as a child. Caption the image with what you'd say to it or them today.

TUESDAY: Sketch a place that both scares you and intrigues you. Caption it with what you would do while there.

WEDNESDAY: Sketch an activity or scenario that gives you pause. Caption it with the first word that comes to mind.

THURSDAY: Sketch a conversation you're anxious to have. Caption it with the first word or sentence you'd use to begin the discussion.

FRIDAY: Sketch a person whom you admire but who intimidates you. Caption it with a question you'd like to ask them.

SATURDAY: Sketch your ideal new beginning. Caption it with "Why not _____?" (And fill in the blank!)

SUNDAY: Sketch whatever you want—or just rest and read the next story.

SENSING
SLOW

On Feeling

A mindfulness exercise (typed adorably in Comic Sans) landed in my inbox at the right time. While the entire list was simple enough, the final prompt caught my eye. I was asked to consider presence through the lens of the body by taking a numerical inventory of what was in the room: things I could see, hear, and so on. Interestingly, the document didn't consider the digital "sense" that can make it impossible to exhale, let alone slow down and take a deep breath.

Now that life often moves between online and offline— the complicated state where our eyes rest on a screen as our heads simultaneously rest on another's shoulder—how are we supposed to feel?

You may feel tired of people asking you to pay attention to things because there's already so much to pay for and attend to, so consider this a forewarning: When slow finally arrives, it may ask to stay with you for a while. It may ask to take up more space than you have to give. It may shuffle around rooms and sift through your dresser or drawers. It may take its sweet time getting ready in the morning, not leaving any hot water, so you're forced to rage quietly during an icy shower. It may tell you a story so drawn out that you find yourself nodding off before it reaches any climactic point. Slow may upend your entire life—but not before embracing you in a deep squeeze and a peck on both cheeks, not before reminding you of your body and your breath.

Sensing slowness in an age of digital demand is a practice I have committed to wholeheartedly. Here is what I've noticed so far:

Slow looks like light—flares, streaks, speckles. It looks like a moment that finds you before you find it: A spotlight appears and brings everything you thought was true into question. You squint, trying to see through the brightness, fighting the urge to turn toward darkness, familiarity—anything softer on the eyes. But what about your heart? It beats with sorrow and drive, experience and hope. Let the light chart a new path if you can't bear to see through the fiery blaze ahead.

Slow sounds like distance. It sounds like the vibrations of airplanes or helicopters sweeping across rooftops and treetops and the satisfying click of heeled shoes hitting a wood floor a few feet away. It sounds like harsh wind drowning out a conversation you're eager to join. There are times when it's hard to break through the noise. Listen for the deep breaths, wet coughs, jagged hiccups, and dramatic sighs. Listen for humanity. Slow is the soundtrack of change.

Slow tastes like the little things—lukewarm coffee, minty lip balm, indulgent snacks, late-night kisses. Take a bite of this, a swig of that. Digest intimate moments privately in a world that asks you to give so much of yourself. Then, gather around a table and notice how the day's aftertaste lingers on your lips. If only our attention lingered a little longer, too.

Slow smells like sweat. It smells like the fumbling last steps of a sprint and summer heat pooling at the base of your hair and neck. It's pungent and sweet, a palate that's both familiar and unsavory. While we're told not to sweat the small stuff, the small stuff can amount to big rewards—especially when *intentionally* working toward something *you* love. Breathe slow in and wear its scent proudly.

Slow feels like everything—but you can only hold so much of it at once. Feel everything writhing, expanding, and coalescing into stories you never knew were inside you. And when you feel like you're about to burst, reach out and touch the world: Run your fingers along the bathroom wall, its damp tiles still sprinkled with iridescent droplets of soapy water. Lean against the cold wall outside your favorite bookstore while waiting for a friend to arrive. Languish in the arms of the one you love while melting into the soft creases of your couch. Slow feels delightful. It feels painful. It feels impossible. It feels miraculous.

Feel the Five Senses

PROMPT

In the digital age, making time and space to *feel* has never been more important. We each move through the world in our own way, so if you need to, adjust any of the following exercises to a sense that feels most appropriate to your experience.

MONDAY: Write about a person, place, or object you want to look at more. How does the experience of actually seeing your chosen subject differ from what you wrote down?

TUESDAY: Write about a song, expression, or voice you often listen to. What about it calms you?

WEDNESDAY: Write about a scent that slows you down. What memories does it conjure, and how do they make you feel?

THURSDAY: Write about a familiar texture, material, or landscape. How does it make you feel—literally and figuratively?

FRIDAY: Write about a flavor or ingredient you slowly warmed to. How does the actual taste differ from what you wrote down?

SATURDAY: Write about laughter as a sixth sense. How do you feel it in your body—in your heart?

SUNDAY: Rest and read the next story.

FROM THE WINDOW

On Looking

Don't forget to open the curtains; you're blocking the light. There—see it? Gaze out of your window long enough and time slows down. Clusters of foliage wave from afar, and below them, little shapes reveal themselves as cars, bicycles, passersby. Scenes and signs of life unfold as far as the eye can travel. Isn't it a relief to watch something other than your reflection?

You spend so much time studying the outline of your body in the dark-screen mirror. When your likeness disappears, the whole world returns. You open tabs and fall into stories: Someone is missing. Someone is achieving. Someone is changing. There is so much to know. Your eyes travel across the surface of articles, captions, social media posts. Sentences stun and stunt you. You wish you'd thought of them first. Having a language for your emotions would invariably make it all better.

But sometimes beautiful words aren't enough—even when they're your own. Sometimes you want to pick up that period in a sentence you wish you never wrote and hurl it across the room like a dodgeball. When the weight of it brings everything down, dust motes from old, crinkled pages of your story burn your eyes. Wafer-thin debris clouds your vision until you blink yourself back into the room. There, in that brokenness, you eventually see remnants of what you couldn't bring yourself to say out loud. You want the words to hang in the balance, no question marks or commas, just open space. Then you slowly try to rearrange them into a better story—no, not better. *Different.* Different will do.

I know this firsthand. I've found myself pulled in a million different directions. I've reached for promises and platitudes, frantically threading words together to make them worthy of others' attention. I've hidden behind beauty and aesthetics to distract myself from the deeply unsettling feeling that I'd made the wrong choice—a feeling I could not filter, mute, or undo with the click of a button.

Now, though, I see the only wrong thing would have been not choosing at all. I've learned that slowness is a drawn-out question, a continuous exercise in curiosity. Slowness is a choice to ask myself: What is stopping me from going deeper—from asking questions at all? From answering them?

There is so much to know—but who says the trees outside my window won't give me the answers I seek? I ask myself this question like a prayer, and I remember that sometimes the only answer is daring to look.

Don't Hide—Seek

PROMPT

Sometimes it feels easier to hide from the world than to face hard truths. The next time you're afraid to really look at what you need, try seeking a new perspective with the following exercises.

MONDAY: Don't hide from your fears—seek a new perspective by reframing what frightens you as a means for growth.

TUESDAY: Don't hide from making mistakes—seek courage by making a visual mood board of images or phrases that inspire you.

WEDNESDAY: Don't hide from change—seek new beginnings by adding a new hobby, outing, or location to your weekly routine.

THURSDAY: Don't hide from the truth—seek your reality by looking in the mirror and saying what you want out loud.

FRIDAY: Don't hide from rest—seek slowness by looking at things (books, movies, photos) that instill a sense of calm at the end of the day.

SATURDAY: Don't hide from your words—seek clarity by writing what you wish for most.

SUNDAY: Don't do anything—besides rest and read the next story.

CAITLIN AND NICHOLAS BARASCH

Writer and Actor, Siblings

As told to Rachel Schwartzmann

Creativity has always been at the center of the Barasch siblings' world. But the writer and actor found themselves at a crossroads when the pandemic took away their busy schedules. As Caitlin worked on her debut novel and Nicholas sought to rekindle a sense of balance, the two took a page from the other's story. "We both struggle with the need for external validation, but I feel like Nick has a clearer sense of how it can be damaging because he's had many years to figure it out," Caitlin says of her younger brother's long-standing performance career. "I think he's much better at saying, 'I'm going to be confident about the work that I'm doing, and even though we all have insecurities, I'm not going to let other people invade my sense of self.'" Since then, Caitlin and Nicholas have sought to find more intention in their careers, and their familial and creative bond has allowed them to learn from one another—in art and life.

"Maybe it's the recovering perfectionist in me, but I always want my storytelling to be everything at once: I want people to be moved in all directions and inspired completely and witness the best thing they've ever seen in their life. For me, it's releasing some control and telling my part of the story—or being the best cog that I can be in a larger story—and hopefully, going forward, continuing to tell stories that I really believe in and not just doing a day's work and picking up my check.

I realized how I was approaching my career—the hustle mentality that actors have of auditioning, looking for the next gig, and constantly working—wasn't serving me. I was figuring that out and letting things occur more organically, but then 2020 felt like a bomb and just blew everything up. But it was welcome. I was forced to come to a complete stop. I almost didn't even have a choice. I was forced to discover what it meant to be Nicholas and not just an actor. That proved to be a super fruitful time, and it's continued. Having gone through the last year or two, I don't believe anymore that it's one or the other—that it's binary. There's another road somewhere down the middle where we can do what we want, achieve what we want, but do it with integrity and hopefully live a little life on the side.

What's the goal? What are we actually working toward? Certainly, in my career, I'm asking: *What do I actually want? What do I want here?* The pandemic is reframing a lot of businesses and how people deal with employees and how people wear ambition and workaholism and the fine line between them. So I hope that the goal now is to prioritize mental health and self-care, compassion and empathy, and all of those big life lessons that connect us."

—NICHOLAS BARASCH

○ ◑ ●

"We were all brought up on storytelling, whether reading, watching TV, listening to the radio, or just listening to one another tell oral stories. We, as human beings, have a familiarity with the way that stories are supposed to function. Seeing everything as a story is useful—but so is remembering that everyone will bring their own conceptions, perceptions, and insights into something, and allowing the story to take different forms when needed.

I define a 'middle moment' as realizing that whatever you've been working toward, or the method you've been using, is no longer working for the moment you're currently in and having to figure out a new way forward. It's the road you reach where it's going in two different directions, and you have to pick one because the road you've just come from is no longer viable.

As Nick said, you can't think of things in a binary way. You've struck upon something interesting: that we will have infinite beginnings, middles, and ends. It seems so crazy to say this as a writer (who has to adhere to a particular structure of beginning, middle, and end)—but essentially, that narrative arc that we think of with our characters, we also think of in our lives. It's almost like we have to divorce ourselves from thinking about our life in a chronological way. This isn't something I have thought about much, but it's a question that I want to ask: *Why are we so hell-bent on creating linear milestones for ourselves?*"

—CAITLIN BARASCH

SPRING

On Beauty

It's always a pleasure to see buds on the branches. When the explosions begin—bursts of verdant green and pink petals overtake the trees, and the world wakes up to its own potential—you'll find me there, waiting in winter's long shadows.

The moment March arrives, I march into the park to kick off a time-honored ritual: blossom hunting. Unlike viewing fall foliage, blossom hunting feels more urgent—even predatorial. I'm starved for sensation. Finding and harnessing this natural magic is the only way I can sustain myself after many colorless months. But beauty cannot survive without breakage, and something within me has quietly broken down over the years.

When I was younger, I saw something and accepted what was before me, but I also could think beyond its edges. A vibrant scene took place, and I would place myself in a stranger's shoes. I would create connections between people, animals, and plants. Plots would unfold, and possibilities would emerge. My sense of self also expanded in these fantasies; all I had to do was let a detail move me enough to keep me moving toward a dream in real life. There is a lot of mileage between then and now: *Now*, I don't dream (as much). I look. I analyze, hunt, document, and ultimately share my findings to show that I can focus on something other than my own interiority. I see the world with all its mundane pleasures and am grateful for them. But sometimes, I wonder if my attention to the present moment has hindered my imagination.

Because in the spring, I am so attuned to beauty that I become rooted in a reality that leaves little room for anything else. I only have enough energy to make sure that what's in front of me is real—and that makes sense, right? There is so much about modern life that makes us doubt our decisions. Our innocence gets swallowed up. Change becomes the undeniable current that runs through everything.

It takes time to discern the clear differences between fostering one's imagination and inflating one's ego—not to see things for our own benefit but to benefit the world by watching it with clear eyes. I think that's the true beauty of spring: taking stock of the present while hunting for small miracles or moments and, in turn, the questions we forgot to ask along the way. What would happen if we looked a little further than what's in front of us? What would we find if we dreamed toward the sky?

Imagine That

PROMPT

The world is full of beauty that calls for your attention, but it's equally important to tend to your inner world. This week, consider the relationship between imagination and attention.

MONDAY: Imagine that time or seasons don't exist in the context that we know today. How would you define a beginning, middle, and ending?

TUESDAY: Imagine that you can understand nature. What would you say or do?

WEDNESDAY: Imagine that your idol is your next-door neighbor. How would you approach them?

THURSDAY: Imagine that more life—driving, walking, sitting—takes place in the sky. What would you look for down below first?

FRIDAY: Imagine that creativity is a concrete cure. What would you want your art to heal first?

SATURDAY: Imagine that the first day of spring grants you an opportunity to live out your dreams for twenty-four hours. How would you spend the day?

SUNDAY: Imagine that the day asks you to slow down. Rest and read the next story.

HOW TO ASK
A QUESTION

On Curiosity

I.

Can you repeat the question?

One of the earliest childhood memories I have about questions is oddly specific: "Did you know that?" from the '90s hit show *Bill Nye the Science Guy*. (I don't remember the episode where I first heard the question, only the distinct cadence of how it was asked.) At that point, I had developed a habit of repeating things, and it just so happened that this question was what I latched on to. It's wild how clearly I can picture sitting in the back seat of my parents' car, driving home from dinner, rambling off, "Did you know that?" in different volumes, inflections, and speeds. Often, childhood is the only time when our questions aren't immediately questioned— only clarified. What a gift to ask something aloud and be met with enthusiasm or wonder (and sometimes a playful side-eye). The saga didn't last beyond the night, but what did last was the feeling: It could be just as much fun to ask as it was to tell.

2.

Why don't you speak up?

I was held back a year in preschool for extreme shyness. My teacher—a whimsical woman who made porcelain dolls on the side—told my parents I (literally) "tiptoed around like a little ballerina." No other description has come close to how I would characterize my childhood gait. Most people knew me as mousy and timid, but there was more to the story: even at a young age, engaging for the sake of making noise seemed pointless.

As I got older, the one piece of feedback I consistently received from teachers was to participate in class. I was fine academically; the insistence that I talk was supposedly for my growth. Inevitably, I *was* asked to speak up and assume a tone deemed acceptable in the classroom: confident, enthusiastic, direct. The latter has become easier over the years, but I still believe that "speaking up" doesn't always equate to saying something worth hearing. And just because I'm quiet doesn't mean I have no interest in asking the big questions. Eventually, I made my work about questions, and as a result, I made my life better for it.

3.

Wait, what did you say?

I constantly run interference—and fall in love—with my inner dialogues. The voice inside is as eloquent and strong as what eventually ends up on the page. The issues arise when I'm nervous: I open my mouth, and the words come tumbling out of order. I blush and sweat, and my voice has a squeakiness that changes the tone of the question, even if it's good. Sometimes asking a question in this state is slightly embarrassing, but I don't stop. I shouldn't. It's more embarrassing not to take a chance.

I've always believed in being considerate before taking up verbal space. But I think I've left a lot on the table. It can be cathartic to ask a burning question, knowing you won't get a concrete response—or any at all. (For instance, nearly every day, I ask myself: Why do my neighbors, who have ample backyard space in the city, choose to have two porcelain toilets—yes, actual toilets—in their garden, each potted with dirt and only the occasional flower? There's a lot to unpack here.) Sometimes the biggest thrill is just putting a question out into your inner world.

4.

Are you asking the right questions?

I launched a small content business with a storytelling component in my early twenties, and aside from asking my interview subjects questions, I also had to get on board with people questioning *me*: What keeps you going (read: why take on something like this so young)? Do you have any advice for others? Why should I invest my talents and time in you?

Looking back, it's clear that this period challenged my ability to see questions as something nourishing rather than alarming. I vividly recall asking questions about the company's survival: What tax classification should I assume? Is it time to part ways with this client or contractor? Do I need to renew my trademark? Will this decision come back to haunt me? Then, one day, after many grueling years of working in circles: Does this make me happy?

Let me repeat that one more time: *Does this make me happy?*

I know that *happiness* unfurls a constellation of words—I've picked stars from its orbit and held on to them until the fire went out—though, over time, I've learned to center it in all I do. This chapter of my life was difficult and instructive: After the uncertainty molded into experience, I learned how to make better choices. I learned how to ask the right questions.

5.

What comes to mind?

People love to hear themselves talk, and this is amplified by the rampant lack of self-awareness in our digital age. Don't get me wrong; having a place to listen and be heard is incredible—but social media is not always the most generative landscape. It takes a lot of our time and energy and, as a result, dilutes our curiosity. We have everything to reach for—but what happens to the furthest reaches of our mind when everything is at our fingertips?

When I run out of questions, it's like I've run out of breath, so I've had to maintain my stamina for interest and empathy. It's easier to trudge through—to trip over sentences and turn questions into statements. Still, without taking time to rest and reflect, I forget the rest of my responsibility: to not speak for the sake of performance. To slow down and be okay with not knowing.

Interviewing people helps me move my questioning in the direction of curiosity versus asking for reassurance, which can be tricky. It seems the older I get, the less I know because stability isn't always on the menu—and I'm hungry. I'm hungry for something other than my words.

6.

Isn't it a simple yes-or-no question?

Answering a question isn't always simple, and sometimes it's even harder to stand by our yeses and noes. We're conditioned to justify or build on our responses to show the world we've given this great thought. That's partly why I used to dismiss rapid-fire questions—*What's your favorite season? How would you describe your style in one word?*—during interviews simply because of my beliefs about conscious pacing. I now know the value of those questions: They don't allow room for overthinking. They can even be fun. (Once, I was asked what swear word best defines my personality—I'll leave my

response to the imagination!) Mostly, they rely on instinct—
and honesty. Simple questions reveal big truths.

7.

What's one question you wish people asked you more often?

I've asked this question a lot over the years, and if I'm being
honest, I initially liked it for its audacity: It stumps people.
But over time, I came to understand that the question gives
people permission to talk about something outside of their
"brand" or "expertise." There is more to their story than how
they appear, their work, or what they make.

When prompted to consider what question they want to be
asked, people often respond with, "How are you . . . really?"
As for me, I wish people would ask why I asked *this* question
in the first place. The answer is much simpler than I used to
think: I ask this question so both of us can get lost in the
sudden silence that usually follows—because when we're lost,
we have a chance at finding something again.

Ask (Yourself) the Questions

PROMPT

Asking questions opens us up to possibility. This week, reflect on—or ask (yourself)—these hard, big, beautiful questions.

MONDAY: *Can you repeat the question?* Reflect on the questions you love to ask.

TUESDAY: *Why don't you speak up?* Reflect on when it feels most appropriate for you to respond or speak out.

WEDNESDAY: *Wait, what did you say?* Reflect on the questions you can't get out of your mind.

THURSDAY: *Are you asking the right questions?* Reflect on the questions that feel important to your life right now.

FRIDAY: *What comes to mind?* Reflect on the questions or ideas that make you curious.

SATURDAY: *Isn't it a simple yes-or-no question?* Reflect on the questions that are fun to answer.

SUNDAY: *What's one question you wish people asked you more often?* Reflect on the questions you'd like to be asked.

TIMESTAMPS

On Process

00:00 The other day, I was in the middle of a bookstore and tried to envision which shelf you would pluck this book from and if the genre could tell you more than I know how to put words to.

1:00 Standing there, several months away from the moment this will be on shelves, I thought of the future even as I wrote about my past, trying to put roots down.

2:00 Somewhere in the present, I struggled to put words down.

3:00 I go back to basics when I need to put words down and can't. I pick things apart. I rhyme.

4:00 *Slow* rhymes with *no* rhymes with *go* rhymes with *low*.

5:00 I'll take the *s* for safekeeping because I'm trying to go low beneath the surface.

6:00 I'm trying to get at something true.

7:00 I'm trying not to flatten this for the sake of being digestible.

8:00 I'm trying to say that slow isn't easy—but it's a story worth telling.

9:00 Typos tell a different story.

10:00 In the early days of writing this book, I accidentally typed *scared* instead of *sacred*, which says a lot.

11:00 I'm not sure if the process should scare you, but I think it should shake you awake.

12:00 I've been writing at a time close to tipping into the next day, so I put these updates here because the truth is most awake in the middle of a sleepless night.

13:00 Darkness is a detail just as much as it is an occurrence.

14:00 In the darkness of night, I squint until I'm eye to eye with tiny terrors: a shadowy ceiling and a cloudy mind.

15:00 Was that the glare of my phone or a light to guide the way forward?

16:00 I've been letting the words and voices of others fill my screen and my mind. They are writing, creating, arguing, begging, hoping.

17:00 Threads unfurl the full spectrum of human emotion. I watch people take the context they need to inform their argument—to be right.

18:00 Writing isn't always the same as righting.

19:00 This might be the most important thing I've learned about writing: The delete button is always there. Everything you say—or don't—is a choice.

20:00 (*Or don't.* Those two simple words chart a path we don't always know is available to us.)

21:00 If a thought sticks around long enough, it'll eventually stick elsewhere.

22:00 Here are the words I chose to write, stuck to this page. Here you are, choosing to read them.

23:00 Yes, *you.* There are only twenty-four hours in a day to process what sometimes feels like a lifetime. I'm glad you're still here with me.

Document the Details

PROMPT

When you're in the middle—of a project, pivot, or process—sometimes the best way to gain clarity is to consider small details. Create space to document the little things with this week's prompts.

MONDAY: Document a moment in nature that brought you back to the present moment. Describe as many calming details about the scene as you can.

TUESDAY: Document a sound. Close your eyes and do nothing but listen to a sound—a nearby voice or song—and, as you do, blindly sketch.

WEDNESDAY: Conduct a check-in. What words or feelings keep coming up for you as you go through this week's exercises?

THURSDAY: Document a conversation. What aspects have stayed with you? Describe as many words, phrases, or emotions as you can.

FRIDAY: Document your reflection. Take note of the items you're wearing, the expression on your face, or the scenery behind you. Describe as many positive details about the scene as you can.

SATURDAY: Document the middle of where you are and write about how it makes you feel. Describe what it means to stand at a crossroads.

SUNDAY: Document nothing. Instead, rest and read the next story.

LYN SLATER

Writer and Activist

As told to Rachel Schwartzmann

Before she was known as the blogger Accidental Icon, Lyn Slater cultivated an established career in social work and academia. But her life transformed when, in her sixties, she launched her fashion blog, which brought her acclaim as a digital tastemaker. Despite her familiarity with constant life change, the demands of the social media landscape ultimately caught up with Lyn, who found herself at a crossroads during the pandemic: remain invested in the online world or pivot toward aspects of the world she felt she was leaving behind? "I started to write a lot more on my blog during the pandemic, and it became more personal," she reflects. "I was protecting my privacy as Accidental Icon and didn't reveal much of myself. But in that writing, I started to talk more about the process of change that was happening for me and what I felt had happened to me before." Today, Lyn has returned to her roots as a conscious storyteller and hopes to create intergenerational spaces that promote connection and community.

"I made the decision that I was going to change my relationship with fashion. I was going to change my relationship with social media. I was going to change how I was thinking about the environment and maybe get back in touch with some of the activism I had done throughout my life until Accidental Icon. I really couldn't continue to live the way that I had been living before the pandemic. We made the decision that we would not buy anything new for our house. We would do recycling and restoration, and organic gardening with native plants. I started to read a lot. I even changed my Instagram approach. I had never used Instagram for writing. At the end of my writing, I asked a question that would make people maybe stop a minute and think, take the time to comment, read other people's comments, and have a conversation.

How do you use your digital time to support what you want to do in your real, human-embodied, everyday life? I use digital in the service of the priorities of my analog life. Since my partner and I moved and retired, our priorities have returned to our partnership, our home, our family, our creative impulses, keeping ourselves healthy, and not harming the earth to the extent we can.

When I was a social worker and professor, I understood my purpose, which was very life-giving. I realized that posting photos on Instagram to sell something is not a purpose. Purpose is something much larger that encompasses your values. It encompasses creativity, new experiences, and leaving something behind in exchange for what you've taken. Starting at the crossroads of what your purpose is—right now—is the beginning question. That spins out in many different ways: *Is your purpose to teach? Is your purpose to change minds? Is your purpose getting people from different generations to talk?* Whenever I've had a purpose, my life has been rich and full and has had a lot of meaning. In recent times, when I was doing something that didn't really have a purpose, I was very unhappy and felt like I had lost my way, did not have a compass, and didn't know what to do.

Life is full of transitions, and they may change your purpose and what you do and what you might value in your life at any particular time. But that's very exciting. It's not something to be afraid of. If you have that attitude that things are not static—they're always going to be shifting and evolving—some people will accept the gift, and some will not and will try to keep their life exactly as it was despite what's happening around them. Looking at a crossroads as an opportunity can lead you to places and experiences you could never even imagine."

ALL, CONSUMING

On Hunger

I tilt my phone at a low angle because I know it's best for this composition. Sunlight flutters in and out of the scene. There are two options: wait for the wind to die down and embrace the soft, flat lighting or go all in on the dramatic shapes and shadows. Either setup will "do well," so I capture both. When I tap my phone's camera button, I recall the many times that people have told me I don't need to make everything so polished, though I can't seem to break the cycle. It's hard to describe the fulfillment I get when an artful arrangement lines up perfectly in frame or a well-worded sentence ties a piece of writing together.

I've made a lot of things for consumption over the years: stories, photos, companies, and food itself. It's not that I'm hungry to make more; it's just that I'd like to make something out of hunger—in other words, I want genuine passion to be my baseline. But there's always so much at play:

We simultaneously are told to rest but can never rest assured when we're told what we're doing is enough. We have an appetite for work and then work to satisfy our appetite.

I have battled these impulses throughout my entire life and want to expand my palate. Because—stay with me here—doesn't it seem like we've devolved into content cannibals? That we create for survival just as much as substance? That we let ourselves be consumed by the expectations and validation of others?

If we are what we eat, how do you feel after feasting on someone's life? After offering up your own on a silver, verified, blue-check platter?

If I created a menu of what I want to make for my life moving forward, it would include messy shared plates topped with inside jokes and weird facts. Main courses filled with more time for literally anything other than screen time. A dessert buffet: bite-size hobbies, sweet thrills, tangy truths, dollops of compassion.

Maintaining our humanity is an all-consuming endeavor, though hunger tends to drive us toward extremes. Taste and texture get lost in a flurry of motion. Then everything is inside of me, and I can hardly recall how it all got there. But I'm starting to metabolize these hard truths. As my stomach settles and my heart races forward, I wish for us all to find a middle ground in our creation and consumption. To nourish ourselves in directions away from societal performance and pressure. To satiate our most uncurated cravings and never tell a soul. To be okay with leaving a mess of crumbs in our wake.

○ ◑ ●

Satisfy Your Appetites

PROMPT

Consider how to satisfy your personal, professional, and creative appetites through mindful consumption, using the following prompts.

MONDAY: Make a "menu" of what you want for your life. Under each "course," write about how this satisfies a particular craving or goal.

TUESDAY: Write about hunger through the lenses of passion and consumption. What are you "consuming" (online and offline), and how is it satisfying your desires?

WEDNESDAY: Create something for your eyes only. What is it like to make something that won't be consumed by anyone else?

THURSDAY: Reflect on your relationship with consumption. What do you like to take in, and how is it positively impacting your life or work?

FRIDAY: Engage in the most "human" thing you think of—like walking barefoot in a patch of grass or relaxing under a cloudy sky. Write about how this experience impacted how you feel regarding creating and consuming.

SATURDAY: Create something tactile (a painting, a sculpture of found objects in your home—the list of options goes on). How can you make meaning out of the mess that comes with these tangible processes?

SUNDAY: Nourish yourself by resting and reading the next story.

SOUTHERN
SKY

On Faith

The Texas sky went on forever. I first became alert to its
power when the town's tornado sirens blared on an overcast
afternoon. As it rang throughout the streets, my mother and
I exchanged horrified glances. Seemingly out of nowhere,
a cluster of ominous clouds gathered above us. We had
recently moved from California to a small suburb outside
of Dallas for my father's job. Everything already felt surreal
here. This "normal" occurrence took my breath away.

I say "normal" because for many others it was. My new elementary school held assemblies to educate us on natural disasters. Every so often, teachers and guest speakers played storm
tapes. As the other kids roared excitedly, I would retreat to
another classroom with one or two outliers who couldn't
handle the footage. Smaller disasters were already unfolding
in dark corners of our house. I didn't want or need to see any
more destruction.

This chapter of my life comes to me in fragments, like lightning striking the ground, slate- and olive-tinted storm clouds passing and parting, sunlight finally streaking through the cracks. Chaos. The siren ended up as nothing but a test—a warning. No twister touched down that day, but I sensed there would be many more storms to weather.

○ ◑ ●

When you grew tired of looking at the big blank blueness, there were other sights to observe. The streets with storybook names held rows of picturesque houses and manicured lawns. Many unfurled vibrant sidewalk-chalk drawings, notes, hopscotch paths, and mazes. This was a place where lemonade stands were expected, and Friday-night football games were revered. Everything was homogenous and hospitable—until it wasn't.

People asked us our names and what church we attended. Our answers didn't suffice. Those innocent interactions sharpened when a few neighborhood kids learned of our Jewish faith. One response, in particular, was scribbled on the asphalt in messy, candy-colored handwriting—and then echoed in a childish drawl by the artist themself: "You can't play with us because you don't believe in Him." (I was in the fifth grade and didn't believe in anything other than my dogs and dolls.)

Despite this, I wasn't alone all of the time. I'd become friendly with some of the girls in my class. But then Elizabeth* arrived and changed everything.

*Name has been changed.

○ ◑ ●

My classmates were drawn to Elizabeth in the way that most kids are drawn to shiny, new things. She was from a faraway place. She had been adopted by a devout family. The list went on, and I joined in their intrigue.

At first glance, Elizabeth was quiet, well-mannered, and very thin. She gladly accepted leftovers from my lunch box. She devoured its contents, and I often stared at her cleaving wrists and collarbone when she wasn't looking. (I think she knew I was.) But then she looked at me, and I felt intense curiosity—kinship, even. The others' fascination waned. Eventually, it was just the two of us.

Letting Elizabeth replace my status as the new girl was a welcome change. And over time, she welcomed me into her private world, sharing stories from her enigmatic past and present. But these intimate exchanges gave way to troubling secrets—out of deference to Elizabeth, they are not mine to tell. I'm not sure I'll ever really know the extent of what happened at her home. I can only tell you what happened in mine.

I can only tell you that when Elizabeth's mother arrived to pick her up from my birthday party and saw our house filled with Hanukkah decorations, she would not come inside. That after I gave Elizabeth a dream catcher for her own birthday, she was no longer permitted to meet me at the playground because the present was "offensive to God." That eventually, Elizabeth told me her mother wished I was dead. I never knew if it was an empty threat or an outright lie, but I told no one and slowly distanced myself from her altogether.

I often think about the many atmospheric ceilings I found myself under as a child. "Chin up," family members would tell me. "You'll settle here and meet new friends. Things will look up soon." I believed them for a while and looked up as far as the eye could travel before I realized I needed to place my faith somewhere closer to home. But where could I truly call home? Was it worth seeking refuge in a house of worship? These questions rattled my young mind because, under the Southern sky, I experienced hate—but I also learned about faith and conviction, however profoundly misguided. Perhaps that's why in the diverse embrace of New York (the city where I now reside), I was able to slowly unlearn what it means to believe beyond the borders of any one religion.

In childhood, I prided myself on looking at something and believing in its full potential. Call that optimism, or naivete, or hope—no word feels big enough to contain the feeling of being alert to opportunity. For that reason, faith has shown itself to me as a slow accumulation of small miracles: evidence that when things are hard, there is a choice to pursue wonder on the edges of the scariest moments. Faith is saying the harrowing stories out loud—acknowledging their impact, remembering the impermanence, finding light after the last page of a difficult chapter. And when all seems lost, faith vacillates between questions and prayers. I don't always know what I'm asking for or who I'm asking it to, but I believe that I have enough agency to find the answers in the ordinary.

Even then, I knew goodbyes were as ordinary as storms. Leaving the South became the only answer that made sense for our family. When we finally arrived in New York many months later, it was dark: the hollow stretch between midnight and morning that feels like forever if you're a kid biding your time. An ink blanket covered the winter sky; a few specks of light cut through its earthen seams. We turned the corner onto Queens Boulevard. I yawned sleepily, my mouth agape and ready to absorb the color and light swiveling out in all directions. As I blinked back into consciousness, I realized it was my first time seeing the Manhattan skyline. Here we were, about to settle into new rhythms in yet another new place. Only now, the sky glittered with possibility. When I looked up, I felt calm. Here I was. *Here* was something to believe in.

○ ◐ ●

Looking back, I started to make good friends in the end: One had dark curly hair and a dimpled smile. She wanted to be a farmer when she grew up. Another friend became a mutual crush; he dropped stuffed animals at our garage door and ran away before I could greet him. Their presence marks the few fond memories from my life down South. If we had stayed there, I think I would have been okay. I want to believe that Elizabeth would've been okay, too.

My last memory of Elizabeth is of her in motion: driving down a suburban block on the cusp of dusk, absently listening to my parents' chatter. The sky was dotted with a few passing rain clouds that mired my reflection as I gazed out of the back seat window. Our pace slowed when we approached a stop sign, and I caught an abrupt movement out of the corner of my eye. There, almost directly beside me, Elizabeth material- ized on a bicycle.

She pedaled lazily. The hem of her pale shirt flowed in the wind. A serene light leak brought the scene in and out of focus. We weren't speaking much by then, but she appeared peaceful when we made eye contact. Years later, I would come to learn how easily pain can disguise itself in a person's smile—at that moment, I only saw a glimmer of this hard truth when Elizabeth raised one arm off her handlebar to wave. Then the car gained speed, taking her further and further out of view. There wasn't enough time to say goodbye as I watched the road blur with the sidewalk—its pavement once covered in pastel messages of fury masked as faith.

Note What You Know

Sometimes charting a path toward faith begins by taking stock of what we know to be true. This week, take note of the present moment using the following prompts.

MONDAY: Note what time it is. How do you feel at this moment?

TUESDAY: Note how old you are. What are some noticeable changes that occurred this year?

WEDNESDAY: Note the season. How does the current environment positively slow you down?

THURSDAY: Note a question you want to ask. What's stopping you from saying it aloud?

FRIDAY: Note where you live. What do you appreciate about living here?

SATURDAY: Note the color of the sky. What does looking up mean for you at this point?

SUNDAY: Note nothing. Instead, rest and read the next story.

PEPPER

On Presence

Do I tell you about her?

I've just finished Ann Patchett's glorious essay collection *These Precious Days*, and closeness is on my mind. Patchett's stories examine time, grief, love, and creativity—the stuff of life—but interspersed throughout are poignant moments featuring dogs: Sparky, her companion; Snoopy, her early creative influence; and neighborhood pups.

I'm drawn to stories that get you to literally close the book, stop stressing out about little things that don't matter, and tend to the things that do—which brings me to the *her* in question. She isn't a dog from a Patchett story but a lionhead rabbit named Pepper, who is a vital part of mine. And while talking about Pepper nearly reduces me to a baby-voiced monster, I think she's worth the space on the page.

So, yes, I'm going to tell you about her.

○ ◐ ●

When John and I decided on pet parenthood, we were a few years into our relationship and agreed that rabbits were a good starting point. They checked the right boxes: small and fluffy (Pepper weighs a whopping three pounds), easy to maintain (we litter trained her), and relatively quiet (save for the surprisingly powerful thumps of frustration and excitement).

On a cool September morning, we sat on the floor in front of what we now call "the blue," a small blue cage that has become Pepper's sanctuary. Amid the blue's confetti-like bedding sat a small cardboard box—which held an adorable and terrified six-week-old bun. We had seen plenty of swoon-worthy photos leading up to her arrival, but in person Pepper was even more striking. She had a smooth black coat and chocolate-brown eyes. Thin streaks of white and tan fur lined the edges of her paws and the insides of her little triangle-shaped ears. When she first lay down, we were thrilled to discover her glowing white belly. We were instantly in love and panic mode. She was so fragile. She fit in the palms of our hands.

The next few weeks marked a crucial bonding period. Pepper would come to know us as the humans who provided every-thing (and liked to get in her face). We saw her shapes expand and contract—true to loaf-like form, she was often round and still, and, when extra relaxed, long and flat. She zoomed around our apartment, getting lost in our stacks of books (read: *I* lost her until I heard the faint sound of chewing from under our coffee table).

John had to travel a lot for work in the intervening months, so it was often just me and Pepper. "You're so round on the ground!" I would half-ask, half-proclaim. She would respond with a slow blink or by "chinning" the items in my lap to claim them. It felt good to have another being there, yet I hadn't felt time operating in such an undetectable way. The trips came and went, and Pepper grew into her big, floppy ears and even bigger personality within what seemed like the blink of an eye. She remained a constant source of presence as the soundtrack to our days changed. Now she's in middle age and continues to ground us in the middle of everything else.

○ ◑ ●

After the initial excitement wanes, some people ask: "So, what does Pepper do when she's not hopping around? Just sit there?" A lot of the time, yes—what's wrong with that?

Pepper has sat through multiple moves, a global pandemic, exhausting presidential elections, a business closure, job changes, a book deal, a marriage proposal, and more. She sits with the emotional turmoil her humans experience almost daily. She sits alongside us as we find ourselves at several crossroads.

I write this essay in a place I know will no longer be my home by the time this book is in your hands. I'm at a point when biology will dictate certain decisions in my life. I don't feel a pull toward motherhood, yet I have a capacity for deep love and care. I'm pulled to the future even when I shift my gaze toward the creature in my charge. How do I navigate these tensions? Where do I put the present realities when the future asks for directions? I don't like to be out of control, but I can't do much about that—so I pick up Pepper's fallen poops and balled-up blanket. I feed her long, fuzzy strands of hay and pinches of pellets. I ask her to "have a seat" and squeal when she throws herself against the wall—feet out, belly up—in response. I live in the present mainly out of demand because Pepper alerts me to her needs and, by default, my own: Feed me. Watch me. Comfort me. Sit with me. *With yourself.* Just for a moment.

Stories about small beings who inspire big presence are all around us. Patchett reminded me of that, and Pepper teaches me all over again every day.

Later, I pluck Mary Oliver's *Dog Songs* off the shelf and situate myself outside the blue. Pepper hops out to investigate. She chins the book cover and nibbles on the edges of the page while I quietly read aloud to myself—and to her (she deserves poetry, just like the rest of us). As Pepper performs these ordinary marvels, I find myself glancing at her nose. The cream-colored fur around it forms the shape of a heart. When I push it close to mine, it flutters with recognition, and I think about how rare it is to be understood beyond words.

Sit in the Moment

PROMPT

This week, meditate on how you can appreciate little moments from ordinary vantage points, from the sofa to your desk chair.

MONDAY: Sit at your desk and reach for any object (other than your computer or work tools) that will bring you calm.

TUESDAY: Sit in the passenger seat and reflect on where you are and where you're currently going.

WEDNESDAY: Sit on the ground and write about what you see or feel from this level.

THURSDAY: Sit next to a loved one and ask them to describe how they feel now.

FRIDAY: Sit alone and ask yourself what this moment means to you.

SATURDAY: Sit on a park bench and count how many people smile or laugh.

SUNDAY: Sit on your bed and rest. (Then read the next story.)

TERESA AND ECHO HOPKINS

Cofounders of Ordinary Habit

As told to Rachel Schwartzmann

Mother-daughter duo Teresa Hopkins, a longtime graphic designer, and Echo Hopkins, a photo producer, are no strangers to the ever-changing pace of creative life. Echo and Teresa eventually found themselves at a professional crossroads and saw an opportunity to build something together with longevity. "We had a strong bond as mother and daughter," Teresa reflects. "We learned how to be with, work with, and listen to each other—which is why I think now it makes per-fect sense to be in business together." Enter Ordinary Habit—their lifestyle goods company whose mission is to cultivate habitual play.

"The middle is where I get a little afraid! I have a challenge, and then I get to the part where I'm not sure which way I'm going to turn—you have to make that decision, which gets a little scary. That's the end of the middle for me because you make your decision, and then you're on your path to finishing it.

People often don't ask why you're doing something: *Why am I putting myself through this kind of stress? Why do I keep this pace?* When you do, that's another daunting moment. I think the question 'why?' is what people don't ask themselves enough."

—TERESA HOPKINS

○ ◐ ●

"The middle is a moment when you've realized that you've figured some things out, but not everything. It kind of signifies the most creative time because you've laid the groundwork and conceptualized an idea. The middle is figuring out all the little details, which is one of my favorite things to do. You're past that initial hump of developing something, and then you're really able to dive in.

I've had to relearn how to make boundaries for time in my life, especially having come from a world of being a producer, on-set, and traveling constantly. We're talking about these little moments you have and can create throughout the day—especially with the availability and connectedness, which can be such a positive thing for so many reasons. But I believe that we're now reexamining how available we are, especially for work. There has been more focus on realizing that pace isn't sustainable. That's a healthy thing to look at a little more closely.

It's really helpful to learn to pause—whether that's something you bring with you into the next phase of a company or even personal relationships and growth. It's taking a moment in the middle to pause and learn from what you did. I think that's where we are right now, and it is simultaneously exciting and terrifying. I've never experienced having those emotions feel so commingled as they are at the crossroads where you can be so excited about what could possibly happen next and learn from everything you've done before then. But you are also taking that blind leap of faith and hoping that the decisions you've made are the correct ones."

—ECHO HOPKINS

PAUSE AND EFFECT

On Pausing

With every action, a reaction. Every cause, an effect. For so long, I've lived in binaries, but the lines have blurred as life becomes more accessible with the click of a button. Whether I am online or not, one idea seems to endure: optimize the pause—make meaning out of interruption.

The middle of the day reveals itself. I take a swig of lukewarm coffee and roll my shoulders. Above, the blazing sun stretches far and wide, its arms reaching across the world as if enveloping us all in an urgent embrace. The light streams through half-open blinds and the questions soon follow: *What have I accomplished today? Do I have enough time? Is it enough?*

With every sunrise, a sunset. The clock ticks on. Dread creeps up like an unexpected gust of wind. The hairs on my neck stand at attention. The afternoon light fades, and the pace slowly shifts. We don't often see the value in delay, but I've

learned how much is achieved in that moment of pause:
I pause a TV show and examine the frozen picture on-screen.
I pause a song and hum the melody to myself as the last sung
word hangs in the air. I pause what I'm reading, and midsentence, a book's words reveal new meaning. I press pause
on societal expectations and make room for new ways to
engage. And once I've slowed down enough, I witness life's
untapped promise.

With every pause, a gift. I reach toward it slowly—like the sun
wrapping its arms around a new dawn.

Take a Midday Walk

The best opportunities for reflection come when we remove the distraction of our devices and take a pause. Create time in your schedule for afternoon walks, and consider the following exercises.

MONDAY: Take an afternoon walk. Pause and notice the details that are the most comforting or familiar to you.

TUESDAY: Listen to your favorite song. Pause the song and write down subsequent, imagined lyrics based on the scenes from today's walk.

WEDNESDAY: Choose a new direction. Pause and consider what details are different from your usual route.

THURSDAY: Do you find yourself walking more slowly or quickly? Do you feel more confident or unsure of your surroundings? Answer these questions by sketching the first thing that comes to mind.

FRIDAY: Call a friend or family member as you walk, and describe the senses that stand out to you. What do you see? Hear? Smell? Take note of the words or ideas that keep coming up in your conversation.

SATURDAY: Take inventory from this exercise. Compile your notes and write a journal entry reflecting on how this practice has changed the quality or direction of your workweek.

SUNDAY: Rest and read the next story.

SUMMER

On Listening

I'm thinking about a long-ago trip to New Mexico. I went to visit my grandmother—an artist whose studio in the desert was a feast for the eyes—because I wanted to interview her for a personal project, but I also wanted to know her better. She is a magical thinker with a singular mind. When I was growing up, she sent me sprawling handwritten letters, inquisitive emails, and one notorious package of small jewelry boxes that, instead of shimmering baubles, held alien-like bug carcasses that she found beautiful.

I've lost track of the full transcript of our conversation, but there is one section that I managed to save. In it, she says: "I've discovered Self with a capital *S*. Being relatively free of family obligations, I've been able to poke and prod into deeper discoveries. I've always been disappointed when going deeper, but at the same time, I relished the opportunity to do so. I feel like there are levels that go deep within that I haven't even touched, even after all these years, so all of my effort is to break through."

No matter how much life experience I gain, it still doesn't feel natural to me to put *self* in front of anything: respect, esteem, care. I can't trust these things will rest on the back of my shoulders alone—that nourishment and understanding begins and ends with me. It's hard to fully listen to the world when it tells me each season requires a unique form of reflection. If history continues to repeat itself, it's safe to say that, for me, summer is a reset of the self—and I appreciate its clear symmetry: Here's what's happened in the last six months, and here's how to go forward for the next.

But before you can reset, you have to reach deep below the surface. Before you can call yourself good, you have to recognize all the ways you are bad. I'm not talking about morality in this instance—I mean skill and effort: the way that hobbies become abandoned because you don't like how the paint has dried on the page, or how relationships can begin on the wrong foot and then, with a lot of work, blossom into something as natural as your own breath. I believe the same is true for the self: Before you become good at being yourself, you have to be bad. You have to do things out of character to see if the lines are worth performing. You have to be a novice before you're all-knowing. You have to listen before you speak. And if no one is saying anything, you have to let the silence speak for itself. You have to live with its deafening, loud insistence to pay attention.

Have you ever experienced a sound just as much as hearing it? One summer, I approached the front door of my apartment building, and my ears started ringing. I whipped my head around to find the source only to realize it was coming from everywhere: the low hum of a few stray wasps making their way out of the hive in the drain spout, the one impatient car on the road. And inside, I heard it when stepping on that annoyingly creaky floorboard and turning on the ancient air conditioner, grimacing as it motored into action. Nothing and no one called out to me specifically, but I felt compelled to wait for instruction. None came, and I realized the next move was up to me. That living was up to me.

When I heard my grandmother's words, I had not arrived in a season of life to recognize their importance. Now that I revisit them in a context of action—writing—I can respond: I don't want to break through—break down. I want to *build* a practice of listening unattached to any public expectation. I want to listen to other, softer calls. I want *self* to preface sustaining, awareness, and less. There is less to wear in the summer, but there are infinitely more ways to change.

At the time of this writing, I've discovered another capital *S* (Slow), though I don't think Self is too far behind. I'll keep looking for the signs. I won't wait for a new season to listen to what life is trying to tell me. For as long as the sun is shining, I'll put myself in front of the world and let it ask me a question—*Can you hear me?*—again and again until I can honestly say, "I hear you loud and clear."

Reflect on Your Reactions

PROMPT

Listening to yourself—and the world—requires shifting from a place of reactivity to reflection. When getting to this place, you'll often find opportunities you might have overlooked. Consider how you can intentionally listen to and reflect on your reactions and impulses with this week's prompts.

MONDAY: How do you react? Write about how your reactions materialize physically, verbally, and creatively in your life or work.

TUESDAY: When do you react? Write about the role timing plays in your impulses in both a personal and professional context.

WEDNESDAY: Why do you react? Write about when an urgent reaction is necessary and who it's meant to serve.

THURSDAY: Where do you react? Write about the online and offline environments that prompt your reactions.

FRIDAY: What do you react to? Write about the people or ideas that prompt your reactions—both the fast and slow.

SATURDAY: How does reactivity inform your relationship with listening? Reflect on this week's prompts, and write about how you'd like to define "reaction" in new life chapters.

SUNDAY: Rest and read the next story.

UNTIL
I SMILE

On Patience

It's hard to remember when I didn't question the ordinary
mechanics of my body. Every inhale crumbles into a sigh;
unexpected gurgles or pops incite worry. After months of this
vicious cycle, I'm ready to focus on other sources of intrigue.
I wander into Prospect Park on an early spring afternoon,
and reverie unfolds in every direction. At the edge of the
infamous "dog beach," a sand-colored French bulldog waddles
through the crowds, its overgrown nails tapping against the
damp concrete. A straggly terrier happily crashes into the
water. One particularly energetic mutt yaps at a nearby turtle
resting on a rock—undeterred, the shelled creature remains
still even as its uninvited companion continues rampaging.

The energy isn't just reserved for the canine variety—the physicality of the people around me is jarring. There is running,
walking, standing, yoga, dancing, laughing, yelling, reading,
jumping, skipping, singing, questioning, howling. As I weave

through hordes of beings—human and animal alike—their presence unsettles me. They greet one another, rest against the budding trees, and wade into the landscape. I don't know any of them and never will, but a specific familiarity courses through the air like wind. I smile at these scenes, but the action somehow feels divorced from my mind.

A faint buzz brings me back to the present. I dig through my tote bag, retrieve my phone, and notice calendar alerts for (perpetually) rescheduled doctors' appointments. I scoff and shove the phone into my front pocket, wincing as it jabs my hip bone. I would rather be alone in the middle of this vast lawn than with someone alerting me to potential bodily threats.

I press on, and as I turn the corner the scene before me is simple but striking. After a recent storm, the park looks healthier and more alive after nursing the effects of a relentlessly gray winter. The grass emits a vibrant shade of green. Trees look fuller; their leaves cast shadows and dappled light on the pavement. I nearly plunge into a puddle but manage to dodge it, not before squinting at my reflection in its murky water. I can only make out my silhouette and distant branches gently swaying behind me. A rare moment of inner calm emerges, and I realize how long I've been waiting for a feeling that I can't define.

It occurs to me then how patience calls to mind being a patient—the act that is supposed to slow us down for our benefit also sounds like the clinical term we ascribe to those who are unwell. Sometimes, that regimented definition is necessary. Still, on the other side of affliction, I want to embrace patience in the same way I welcome these little moments—out of necessity but also in awe. Because when you are sad, smiling feels like you're ripping a part of yourself open. When you are hurt, exposure to the elements feels like an invasion. But with enough willingness, I've started to remember that when I'm doubled over in anguish—waiting for the pain, fear, or despair to pass—there will come a time when I have the capacity to be doubled over laughing instead.

For now, I let seasons remind me that time passes, and every-thing changes. I let nature show me our ability to heal after hurting. I let green grass and little moments of connection move me until I'm back in my body and know that something extraordinary is still possible—until I smile. I prescribe myself patience and hope for the best.

Prescribe Yourself Patience

PROMPT

Patience is both an art and a practice—but once it's mastered, the world opens up in ways you never imagined possible. Prescribe yourself a small dose of patience this week.

MONDAY: Are you standing by for an overdue message or email? Wait for a response. Consider why you've attached a level of urgency to it, and write about how it feels to slow down.

TUESDAY: Are you creatively blocked? Brainstorm a project or idea. Keep a list of words, phrases, or symbols that come to mind. Let those patterns forge a path forward.

WEDNESDAY: Are you looking to break out of old habits? Try something new, and don't measure how quickly you do it. Write about how it makes you feel.

THURSDAY: Are you hungry for something new? Make a favorite meal and slowly savor it. As you eat, reflect on what motivates your desire for this experience.

FRIDAY: Are you itching to travel? Start small and go for a walk. Observe the sights and reflect on what it means to move with intention.

SATURDAY: Are you hoping to slow down? Curb your pace by taking slower steps, and sending slower responses. What ideas come to you in the space between thought and action?

SUNDAY: Are you hoping to find stillness? Rest and read the next story.

MOUNTAIN
TIME

On Movement

The plan was to visit Mount Rainier in July. Two years into the pandemic, John and I were constantly unsure of our proximity to danger. We lived in fits and starts, tracking our movements against the scale that tipped in our favor one day and left us hanging the next. Because of this, the vastness of Rainier almost didn't compute.

It had been an unusually snowy season at the park. Elsewhere, summer presented itself in a blaze and a widespread heat wave enveloped the country. But at Mount Rainier the trails were still dotted with patches of ice, and wildflowers struggled to break through the soil. The closer our departure became, the more the experience was framed as picturesque, nourishing, necessary. Think of the flora and fauna: a feast for the eyes. ("The chance of seeing a black bear is close to zero," John added when I expressed hesitation about certain wildlife. "You're more likely to see a marmot!") Phones and computer screens were shoved in my face: Look at its beauty. Feel something.

I did feel something. I felt like I was free-falling.

○ ◑ ●

For many years, movement imbued our shared life: a yearlong resolution to visit a new city in America every month. Packed itineraries abroad in Stockholm and Paris. Weekend getaways to upstate New York. Family gatherings in Union Beach and Corrales.

If I think about all of the environments John and I found ourselves in, steep terrains always seemed to stand out: the hilly vista points in Big Sur, a snow-laden Stratton, terra-cotta-tinted dust caking our shoes from the Jemez Mountains, the winding cobblestone roads ascending to Montmartre. Even our neighborhood has "slope" built into its name. All of this to say, we were happiest when we were going up. John and I had come to understand this direction as a reward. We strove to reach—*be*—the top of wherever we were in the world.

Travel was, at once, a big luxury and a small mercy—a chance to disengage from our career ambitions. Despite this, we found ourselves falling prey to the usual trope of millennials unable to unplug. Climbing the steps of our hotel, we'd glimpse at our phones for unread Slack messages or Instagram notifications, admonishing one another with a knowing sigh. We didn't *want* to work but had difficulty imagining a routine without a quick inbox refresh. It was a reflex.

In this way, movement became medicine. We wandered through new locales with renewed intention, knowing our time there was limited. We visited historic sites and ogled each other during romantic meals. It was a healthier use of our energy, though every moment was enveloped by sensory overload, leaving little room to process how we—*I*—actually felt.

I often wove through crowds holding John's hand and digging in my pocket for stomach medicine as inner butterflies turned into violent waves. I let my reddening cheeks and nervous sweat serve as a natural blush and sheen for photo ops. I folded my anxieties in thirds, tucked between flea-market treasures and travel toothbrushes. They fit neatly in my carry-on for a while.

A tingling sensation echoes from the tips of my fingers to the soft middle of my palms—one thousand pins and needles pulsing. Then, a thickness swells in my throat, reverberating outward as hot hives emerge in waffled patterns up and down my neck and chest. My red skin gives way to red-hot nausea, shooting down to my stomach and souring it entirely. This cycle can happen once in a while or once a night. It doesn't matter. I'm always depleted by the end.

Anxiety has shown itself as a full-body experience, one that I've been navigating in some form since I was a child. Various things trigger me. Some days, I'm horrified by the thought of breaking routine, even if it means meeting a new friend for lunch. Other times, I can't fathom being out at night, feeling claustrophobic in dark restaurants, surrounded by hordes of people and the din of clinking glasses. Context aside, my remedy remains consistent: I hug my knees to my chest, demand to be alone, and wait.

I believed I knew what to expect when these warning signs emerged—and I did, for some time. Then, a few weeks before we were set to leave for Mount Rainier, anxiety played a new hand.

○ ◑ ●

I once described my lifestyle as propulsive—there was always a reason to keep moving. But as spring unfurled blossoms on trees, my instincts were tested after years of enforced stillness. Let me set the scene: Two boxes of tissues and an electric thermometer sat lamely on the edge of our bed. John and I had reached the end of our first encounter with COVID-19. He fought off fevers and prayed for his sense of smell and taste to return. I was the luckier of the two of us—no fever, a slightly sore throat—and would test negative just a few days after the initial onset. But to catch it after so much diligence felt like a personal failure.

Light streaked through our bedroom window. (Good weather adds insult to injury when you're relegated to staying indoors.) I stood at the foot of our bed basking in a small patch of sun, and almost suddenly, pressure gripped my arms and chest.

"Something's wrong," I whispered. "Something's not right."

John peeked over from his iPad; concern and familiarity registered in his expression. "Try to remember that you're vaccinated and boosted and always masked," he began slowly. "You got it, but it's almost over. And if something were wrong, you wouldn't be able to stand and talk to me. You're gonna be fine."

But logic was no match for fear. I shook my head violently and waved him off. The pressure intensified, and images of illness and despair flashed through my mind like rapidly changing channels. Every part of my body felt activated: I pointed my toes and flexed my fingers. I bit my lip and scratched at my chest. I lay down and stood up, repeating the motion like a robotic toy. Movement had once added excitement to my life, but in that moment it became full-blown terror—I couldn't stop moving.

As I paced the length of our apartment, shuffling quickly from one side of the space to the other, I understood that I was no longer in the driver's seat of my own body. I kept my eyes downcast toward my phone, which played episodes of a cult '90s sitcom on repeat. For hours, I watched and walked, my feet barely leaving the floor, small tears in my socks expanding like craters. Audience laughter poured out of the tiny speakers, drowning out my frustrated groans. A thin layer of sweat gathered at my hairline. Still behind his screen, John tried to catch my eye. He was silent, knowing by now that no words would offer comfort. I looked in his direction every so often, flushed with shame. He smiled at me sadly.

Twelve hundred steps and nearly five hours later, I gasped with relief. The tide had finally turned. I lowered myself onto our bed and sat calmly without stirring for the first time that day. My eyes met John's, but we were at a loss for words. "Well," I said, breaking the silence after a minute or two. "That's new."

What followed marked a clear turning point: aversion to eating full meals for fear of getting sick. Emotionally detaching during an attempted family celebration. Literally running out of museums, theaters, public spaces in a panic. A general inability to participate in the world. Life thrummed around us, but I retreated further away from everything and everyone until leaving the house was the only accomplishment I could lay claim to. As our trip grew closer, I was sure of only one thing: I would not make it to the airport.

The lone window in my home office looks out on a tree-lined Brooklyn street. When summer arrives, explosions of greenery beckon city dwellers outside. As it rains, the shimmering droplets cleanse the streets like a spiritual bath. Not long after the incident, I sat next to my whirring fan, taking in these seasonal delights. I was waiting.

Outside, the branches swayed calmly, guided by the silent lullaby of summer wind. Then, a flash of red and a quick glimpse at a cardinal charging across the ceiling of leaves, disrupting their rhythmic motion. I'd grown accustomed to these small shocks, knowing how abruptly things can change—how much a single outside force can shake our sense of stability. It happens every day.

Humans aren't granted wings in this life, yet I desperately wanted to rise above the weight of my private world. *Is it freeing to flutter over the tops of the spaces that confine us—protect us? To know your direction with no guideposts—just a vast open sky? What does it feel like to soar?*

The room refocused as I clicked on the appointment link and waited for my first therapy session to begin. The initial hour was a primer, laying out how to best use our time together. My therapist invited me to share how I might have arrived at this point. Anecdotes gushed out like an open fire hydrant spewing water onto the streets. I finally admitted that this was my first time seeking support.

"You're ready to feel something different," she asserted kindly.

I shifted in my seat and looked away. The trees had returned to their tranquil state, soaking in afternoon light. There were no cardinals, robins, or pigeons in sight. My eyes roamed higher: beyond the treetops, soft clouds; beyond that, sky and stars; beyond that, anything and everything. *This is the highest point I'll reach for a while*, I thought as images of fog-laden mountaintops appeared in my mind.

There was nowhere else to go. There was nowhere else I'd rather be.

"Yes," I said, mostly to my on-screen reflection. "I want to try."

"What does anxiety feel like?" someone close to me asked. "Like inside your head?"

I didn't have the words as July crashed into August and then a new season altogether—if I did, they were submerged in the nauseous trance that consumed me for days. If I did, they hid in the "sick bag" I made in case I couldn't calm myself down. If I did, they were drowned out by the sound of heart palpitations and heavy sighs. But I have the words now.

I would tell them that anxiety makes me a liar. When people ask how I'm doing, I want to tell them that I feel like collapsing into myself, but instead say that "I'm busy; fine." The latter is easier because who says I owe them the truth? But then, when the corners of my mouth produce a sharp pain from a day of forced laughter, I remember that anxiety feels like a betrayal. I'm not sure I can trust that my mind and body will ever be in sync.

Anxiety feels like an electrical current sapping my imagination and draining my social battery. I liken it to having a sixth sense: perpetual crisis. There is intrusion and destruction, and the thoughts get so loud that hunger and fullness become weaponized: *You will fall apart*, it says. *Everything will fall apart. You will expel your breakfast, lunch, and dinner, then your love, confidence, and hope, until there's nothing left inside but fear.* It turns out that fear is a potent seed. When I've spewed the last drops, I envision whatever's left mixing with my stomach bile, fusing into toxic soil for more trouble to grow.

I would tell them that, at its worst, anxiety pulls my soul
out of my body, using it as an energy source to mess with
life's circuitry. Everything loses its wonder. Not a single
light switch in sight will turn on. So I fumble around in the
darkness, straining to remember another way of moving
through the world.

○ ◑ ●

I never doubted my ability to keep up with John, but occasionally his confidence overwhelmed me. I watched him move
through the world with genuine self-awareness during our
earliest travels together. Each time I became more conscious
of my shortcomings—my anxieties. But I was younger then,
and at that point, flaws seemed like opportunities to rewrite
a more convenient story, one I thought the rest of the world
wanted to hear: *Go this way, act like this, see this place, be this
person—and whatever you do, make sure you are at the top of
your game.* My relationship with movement grew increasingly
complicated, motivated by societal obligation just as much
as curiosity about the world. I embraced an energy I couldn't
always trust was pushing me in the right direction.

Eventually, I slowed down. In many ways, I thought achieving slowness was the most accessible form of enlightenment.
It was advertised to me as being on the same level as well-
being, understanding, equilibrium—but when I started to
claim it fully, I recognized just how nuanced it is. As much as
slowness encourages us to pay attention to possibility, it also
shows us exactly where we are. And those places aren't always
what we expect.

For so long, anxiety has occupied more than the periphery of my days. It's become a form of slowness all its own, invoking a time zone that causes me to move through life at a different pace. Because of this, I've learned to measure time differently. Love, too.

Love blooms in motion but matures in stillness: the deep, uncharted territory that can't be tracked by apps or miles. Love is out of frame: in the blurred edges of our best photos, my lips pecking the top of his head. Love is taking one step forward—and then many steps back—to build a life that moves you across time and space.

On the morning of the tour, John promised to send me updates, but when the last of his cell service vanished, so did his texts. Having stayed behind in Brooklyn, I stirred in our apartment, as the air grew thick with longing and exhaustion. I couldn't sit still, knowing it was mountain time.

Afternoon clouds gathered overhead, offering relief from the heat as I wandered into Prospect Park. People gathered in every corner: couples giggling on picnic blankets, shrieking children drowning out the pleas of young camp counselors, panting runners flying into view and then suddenly vanishing around the bend. Watching them, I wondered what was roiling beneath the surface of their flushed faces. I thought about how we slowly summit our lives—that universal insistence to keep putting one foot in front of the other even when the peak seems out of reach. Later, John would share visual evidence of what happens when we do: stunning film photos of cascading waterfalls glistening like holy water, light leaks adding a unique texture to earthen landscapes. My absence was noticeable, though it felt softened by the angelic glow bathing the fir trees.

Maybe this story would have been easier to tell had I seen these small wonders up close, but perspective also reveals itself in unexpected places—ones that erupt, erode, endure. Ultimately, I couldn't follow John on those trails, opting instead for a path toward recovery (a hike I will be on for the rest of my life). But despite the long road ahead, I found myself on solid ground that day: walking alone in the small patch of wilderness we call home—anxious heart beating in my chest, thoughts racing to the top of a mountain deep within—missing him.

Move (with) Your Mountains

Overcoming challenges can require slowness—and acceptance. To move mountains, first consider how to move *alongside* them with these daily prompts.

MONDAY: Hike your heart—write about how you're feeling from head to toe.

TUESDAY: Write about what being on top of the world feels like for you.

WEDNESDAY: Write about what rock bottom feels like for you. What steps do you want to take to feel something different?

THURSDAY: Write about what it feels like to move through a challenging period. How (quickly or slowly) do you move?

FRIDAY: Move your thoughts from one place to another. If you've been keeping them to yourself, say them out loud; if you've been writing about them, draw them instead, and so on.

SATURDAY: Write about how you move through challenging periods alone versus with others. What feels the most comforting to you, and what would connection look and feel like for you in these circumstances?

SUNDAY: Rest and read the next story.

ONE SMALL TRUTH

On Living

No matter my age, I've always felt annoyed when someone I love asks me to take a deep breath. It wasn't until recently I realized they were really just asking me to take a moment to deeply enjoy my life.

○ ◑ ●

Implement Small Slowdowns

PROMPT

Despite our best efforts, sometimes life moves fast. This week, slow down, take a deep breath, and take a moment out of your day to . . .

MONDAY: Simplify your to-do list by assessing what action items can wait.

TUESDAY: Mute distracting apps on your phone.

WEDNESDAY: Set allotted "do not disturb" hours that allow for midweek rest.

THURSDAY: Reflect on what's essential for you to share on social media.

FRIDAY: Text or email someone who matters to you.

SATURDAY: Indulge in your favorite snack.

SUNDAY: Rest and read the next story.

End

DREAMS

On Endings

Our plane flew through a clear blue sky, then swiftly took a nosedive toward the sea. Terror and acceptance coursed through my body. The sun shone brightly through the cabin windows. When we hit the water, my eyes opened. *What had conjured such an awful dream?* As I registered the morning sun in my bedroom, I lost my train of thought and the horrifying image faded away.

You lose your train of thought for a single moment, and it can still upend your entire day. But what about when you lose yourself in your dreams entirely? This wasn't the first time I had dreamt of flying peacefully only to meet a horrifying end. Following a period of intense professional focus, I had decided that pacing myself took precedence over performance. I'd closed my business and cut myself from a network and net worth—creating reasonable concerns. Still, my literal dreams and nightmares—crashes, explosions, reunions, and forgiveness—left a more visceral impact than my daydreams and ambitions. The full spectrum of the human experience played out in my subconscious like an episodic series. Then they ended, and reality began once more.

We collect life dreams like trophies, rare gemstones, or followers. They can be confused with achievements to reach for rather than ideas to reflect on. I should know. I was a big dreamer—I wanted everything—until I realized I had been sleepwalking for nearly a decade. Because when I dreamed about the future, I wasn't awake to what was being lost in the moment: time, energy, attention. When I finally woke up, I found myself at the end of the road. The expectations I had set, the dreams I was chasing, would never sustain my happiness. Work was always supposed to support my life rather than consume it.

People my age and younger often scoff at the notion of dreaming about labor. Their disdain is just the beginning for me. Put simply, I'm tired. I'm tired of ambition—at least the hustle-clad narrative of it we've been sold. I'm tired of reading about it. I'm tired of analyzing it. I'm tired of questioning it. I'm tired of talking about it because, in some regard, it means I'm talking about myself. So, at least for a little while, I'm shutting my mouth. I'm closing my eyes, resting from ambition and letting it drift away in the same way I doze off.

In sleep, I've learned about a different form of work. I've let what's buried deep inside reanimate as ethereal lessons or reminders: I'm on a plane departing and arriving; I'm running away; I'm reconnecting with someone; I'm seeing things in a way that the days' distractions often obscure; I'm living. Dreams have deepened my relationship with time in waking life. They show me how fast it goes.

With age, I've learned to appreciate that *end* is found in things outside work: fri*end*, m*end*, compreh*end*, t*end*. We all do our best to recognize and care for what we have, personally and professionally, for as long as possible. We all have something we're holding on to. In this way, endings are the one thing we collectively share. Nothing lasts forever: not a dream, not a job, not a story.

While I've never been good at closing little things—doors, drawers, windows—I'm much better at knowing when it's time to close a significant life chapter. Though that doesn't mean the process is always easy. In recent years, my endings have looked like falling apart and have felt like falling from the sky. But at this moment, everything is still. Night has fallen, and when I finish writing, I will try to fall asleep. I will close my eyes and find myself at the edge of a day and a dream. I'll open myself up to something more. This isn't a story so much as a promise. Read these words, and help me keep it.

Dream a New Dream

PROMPT

How would you define your relationship with dreaming?
Consider these prompts as you reflect on your dreams in
waking life, sleep, or both.

MONDAY: Write about your earliest definition of *dreams*.
How has it changed over time?

TUESDAY: Write about a dream that came to a natural end. How did you feel or what did you do when it
was over?

WEDNESDAY: Write about a dream you "woke up" from.
How do you think it would have ended had it continued?

THURSDAY: Write about a dream you let go of. What
were the circumstances, and how do you see the
decision now that there's been some distance?

FRIDAY: Write about dreams and ambitions. What are
the main differences between the two?

SATURDAY: Write about daydreaming. How does it serve
you just as much as distract you from your goals?

SUNDAY: Rest and read the next story.

SPACE BEYOND THE STARS

On Uncertainty

I have a hard time falling asleep, and tonight, I find myself thinking about my childhood. Everything and nothing has changed. Back then, I would lie awake gazing at the glow-in-the-dark outer-space stickers that blanketed my ceiling. Crescent moons and constellations winked at me in the quiet of the night; in turn, I would squirm around in bed and chat with them. It became a comforting ritual. The space between me and those tiny decorative objects felt immaterial—it was as if I could reach into the darkness and pluck them from my make-believe sky. I soon realized that I couldn't, but I didn't allow myself to believe that the distance between what I wanted and where I was couldn't be overcome. These moments were my earliest experiences understanding what space could be beyond the stars.

Eventually, I understood that twinkling night skies can still give way to dark days. I learned to adapt to the norms of whatever space I inhabited: sterile conference rooms, hole-in-the-wall cafés, opulent dinner parties. I entered a room and made myself part of its galaxy.

It's easy to do that living in New York, a city that sparkles with confidence. In packed spaces, I catch my distorted reflection in golden champagne flutes. I toast with rising stars and crane my neck to find the exit sign. There is hardly time to think about what life could look like beyond this space, making it difficult to recognize myself outside its boundaries. It's even harder to accept that the space I've worked to create my entire adult life might be the very thing that could swallow me whole.

After the decorative solar systems came emojis, hearts, and likes: The digital space unfurled a nebula of things to reach for. It was a space I found myself in slowly and then suddenly, until it became all-consuming. Now, it takes more than it gives. It demands a perpetual statement of proof that we're worth listening to—that we have something interesting to say.

Each time I scroll, I consume the carefully curated frames at my fingertips. People I follow depict different scenarios about value: Some share thoughts about making the most of the spaces we inhabit. Others share a behind-the-scenes look at their search for a space that furnishes their lavish lifestyles. Then there are those who make their investments in emotional real estate—igniting a conversation with their followers—in hopes of creating space for satisfaction beyond material gain. Over time, I've learned to tread delicately between these extremes while, true to form, still ending each day lying wide awake. Storybooks and childhood imagination would keep me up at night as a girl. Now I'm kept awake unpacking my daily travels through a space that exists in the four corners of a screen.

○ ◑ ●

Lately, darkness has taken on the consistency of loss. I pull my blanket closer as if it'll be absorbed into the cosmos of my bedroom. Unable to fall asleep, I shift my gaze from the ceiling fan whirring overhead to the tiny cracks between the blinds hanging over the window. If I squint closely, I can make out the few visible stars dotted throughout the night sky—but I won't reach for them as I once did.

A faint buzz brings my attention back to my body. The sensation continues until I garner enough energy to address my phone, which has been vibrating face down on my stomach. The light from its screen emits a harsh glow. It pulls me in with a gravitational force—my very own comet of distractions. I pick it up, ignoring the message, and silently scroll through motivational prompts on my social feed, which encourage reflection along the lines of: *How do we hold space for others? How do we encourage space for hard conversations? How do we create space for new beginnings?*

Questions like these transcend the screen and make their way into my subconscious. They strike me as I wind through congested streets. They rewrite themselves across my anxious face as I hurry past strangers who scowl at me for invading their personal space. After spending nearly two decades here, I know that New York may instill a grand state of mind, but it's not comfortable. It creates discourse. It forces awareness. Slowly, I've found the courage to verbalize these feelings of uncertainty about my role in this space—this city.

So, I decide tonight is as good a time as any to acknowledge this awareness in a space I know won't betray me. I open the Notes app on my phone and begin to type:

You can see clouds in the sky, feel the wind in your hair, taste the sweat running down your face as you make your way through crowds of people, and fight for your space in (or on) line—for your seat at the table. You can see the things that make up the space you know best with your eyes, but that doesn't mean you always want to face them with your heart. I'm circling the entrance to a space that I haven't faced in a long time: one that is entirely unknown.

I examine what I've written, my chest rising and falling as I swim in each sentence. When my eyes reach the surface of that last word, I allow myself the pleasure of a long-overdue exhale—I say it slowly: "Unknown." My voice cracks. It's an imperfect delivery to an absent audience, but I've whispered life into the doubt that has consumed me. And after hearing the word out loud, for the first time in a long time, the space around me feels infinite.

Embrace Blank Space

PROMPT

Uncertainty can open the door to opportunities and places we hadn't thought were available to us. Embrace the blank, unknown spaces in your life with this week's exercises.

MONDAY: Embrace the blank page. Write a list of uncertainties that are on your mind. How does it feel to put pen to paper?

TUESDAY: Embrace a blank canvas. Draw in a color palette that best captures your state of mind. What visual patterns emerge?

WEDNESDAY: Embrace a blank wall. Cover it with images or objects that make your space feel like home. Which people or places in your life come to mind?

THURSDAY: Embrace a blank itinerary. Fill an upcoming day in your calendar with activities unattached to productivity. How do you think you'll describe your mood by the end of that day?

FRIDAY: Embrace a blank screen. Only fill your social feeds with content that adds value to your life. Do you find yourself engaging more or less?

SATURDAY: Embrace a blank answer. Respond with "I still don't know" to a question you've had difficulty answering. How is it clarifying to verbalize the unknown?

SUNDAY: Embrace a blank day. Rest and read the next story.

STILL
HERE

On Loss

Plenty of foliage enveloped my grandmother's New Mexico property—giant cottonwoods, clusters of spiky cacti—but what always heartened me the most after the cross-country flight were the trees of heaven. Before these leafy canopies came into view, chestnut dirt coated the sides of the truck as my family rolled down Corrales Road. Each time we turned onto the driveway, my grandmother beamed at me. "Here we are, honey," she sang as my father chuckled in the driver's seat.

Prior to my parents' separation, we considered leaving Texas to join my grandmother in the Land of Enchantment. After much debate and other circumstances, we relocated to New York instead. I was devastated by the missed opportunity—I'd already enrolled at a local middle school—though it worked out in the grand scheme of things. New Mexico became a second home predicated on rejuvenation rather than confinement. So when my grandmother decided to put her house on the market many years later, I was gutted. There were logistical considerations that made sense—still, she had been there for decades, and my father had joined her after a tumultuous twelve years in New York. All of us were tethered to her New Mexico home in some way.

Weeks before they moved, I sat in the front passenger seat of my father's truck. A football game blared on the radio, and his team was on the precipice of a rare win. He growled in frustration when they didn't accomplish what was needed on the field. I remained silent from carsickness and nostalgia while my now-husband tried to appease us both from the back seat.

"Come on!" my father wailed as the announcer relayed another misstep.

Somehow the team triumphed in the end, and my father was ecstatic, especially given their long-term losing streak. Context aside, I had always admired my father's loyalty amid loss. He knew it well at that point in his life but never let it get in the way of moving forward. He never stopped rooting for his people—no matter where they were. That attitude would once again prove valuable for our family: By the spring, my grandmother would move to the West Coast, and a few months after that, my father would begin anew in a sleepy southeastern beach town.

Once, my father referred to New Mexico as "a soft landing," and he was right to call it that. It cradled us during breakups and breakdowns. It welcomed us from other places that demanded energy we could no longer spare. I think that's why this loss affected me more deeply than others. All of us were much older. These people I had depended on were already far away, and the distance between us would continue growing. There was less of everything—time, money, promises—and still so much to lose.

Over the years, I've lost sight of what loss is supposed to look and feel like and how I'm supposed to navigate it. I've tried to assign texture and temperature to it, like weather. I've attempted to prepare for its arrival the way one initiates a seasonal wardrobe swap, schedules vacation days, or stockpiles medicine before a suspected outbreak. Loss reveals a more complicated truth when I least expect it: It shows me what was there, often more clearly than in the moment I had lived. Loss is the ultimate punishment for refusing to be fully present.

I never actually lived in New Mexico, so I can't claim it as my home—but for a while, it was a place that oriented my family and me toward each other, and maybe that's what home is. In any case, we know to point our familial compass beyond geography. Our stories keep us bound to land and love. My phone alerts me to a trove of memories together: afternoon walks along the Rio Grande, setting up holiday snack stations, viewing works-in-progress inside my grandmother's art studio. I haven't lost the pictures in my mind. I'm still here: in my father's car listening to a game that I don't know the rules to, cruising down the highway, watching distant storm clouds roll over the mountains.

○ ◑ ●

Write a Lost-and-Found List

It can be difficult to put things in perspective as losses happen in real time. Sometimes, it's helpful to write it all down. Try listing your losses—and correlating finds—and follow this week's prompts as you assemble your list.

MONDAY: Decide what losses and finds you'd like to focus on—personal, professional, creative, and so on. Begin a list with the chosen area(s) in mind.

TUESDAY: Write about a loss and what you found in the space it created afterward. Was it what you were expecting?

WEDNESDAY: Write about a loss that ultimately helped you find or understand yourself better.

THURSDAY: Write about a place where you had to start over. What or who did you find there?

FRIDAY: Write about a person you lost or grew apart from. Who did you find in this individual's absence?

SATURDAY: Write about something you're willing to lose and what you hope to gain in its place.

SUNDAY: Rest and read the next story.

NICOLE LOHER

Climate Communicator, Researcher, and Lecturer

As told to Rachel Schwartzmann

Sometimes living authentically requires closing a chapter. Nicole Loher, a revered Tumblr-style blogger, had long questioned fashion's often-volatile working environments and collective impact on the world. After spending years working in the fashion industry, Nicole turned down a life-changing move to Paris, ending a career chapter and paving the way for a new beginning in the climate sector. This experience helped Nicole see that recalibrating our relationship with pace can be channeled in more conscious directions. A self-proclaimed minimalist, she also believes in using her digital platform responsibly, and with that comes uncomfortable, necessary boundaries—online and off.

"For me, most things have a game plan. I have a lot of anxiety about the unknown, so I try to create support systems for everything I do. On the flip side of that: I've been let go from a job, and I've had to end a relationship that wasn't working, and those are some unknown unknowns that we can't really predict.

A lot of people try to reason with why things end. The questions, more or less, we should be asking are: *What positive thing happened from this? What can I learn from this?* The greatest trait you have is resilience, framing things psychologically as optimistic when looking at endings. *How do we reframe something potentially sad or traumatic as a new beginning? How can we look at this end as a new beginning? What is the new beginning out of this?*

Work endings are always sad, but beautiful; without mine, I wouldn't have been able to grow in my career the way I did. It honestly wouldn't have led me to the point of finding the climate field. The idea of jumping off the treadmill of life is scary, but I also think there is beauty in trying to figure out something new and in learning. You learn a lot about your process in ending things and then restarting. I think the difference between when I was on social media in the Tumblr years is that the intent was there for me to be successful and create a career for myself, which I ended up doing. In the flux of the last few years, I lost that. I was haphazardly sharing my life and all the things that go along with it. It did lose its intention. That time offline helped me go through: *Who should I be following? What am I using social media for? What is the message that I want to be sharing—if any?*

People need to give themselves more credit and allow a little more elasticity for how they look at themselves in the world—just slow down for thirty seconds. That's enough time to test the waters. It has only benefited me in my mental health and how I view life. Other people could probably benefit from a slower pace, too."

A LIVING
ARCHIVE

On Taking Stock

I've always strived to cultivate environments that reflect my
sensibility. As a young person, I spent hours arranging floor-
to-ceiling displays of film strips and fish-eye photos. I thrifted
mannequins and dressed them in hand-painted T-shirts.
Floating shelves housed diaries filled with multimedia
collages made from travel brochures. Fairy lights or vintage
lamps led the way in and out. My childhood rooms were
sensory dreams, but as I grew up, my self-expression moved
online. There, I built virtual homes. I found inspiration in
internet visual trends. I wrote on web pages rather than journal pages. I managed to find some solace offline, though.

Early in my career, I visited countless artists' and designers'
studios. Their processes—often rooted in tactile methods
and traditions—kept me grounded in the real world even as
I spent so much time plugged into the digital one. The studios ranged from corporate showrooms to fluorescent-lit

basements, but almost all featured one distinct element: a mood board. Some mood boards took up entire rooms, and others added a bit of flair to nondescript corners. Over time, it became hard for me to detach these boards from their chic environments. I didn't recognize it then, but mood boards also presented themselves as status symbols, communicating the relationship between artistic vision and commercial success. I watched some of my favorite creative professionals pose in front of floor-to-ceiling boards, donning their seasonal inspiration, often featuring glossy magazine pages and fabric swatches. The aesthetic of it all hooked me just as much as the final creations.

Eventually, the less glamorous demands of hustle culture caught up with me, and as I contemplated what direction to move in next, I was flooded with memories of the time spent with makers in their spaces. Time spent marveling at the details that made their visions come to life and reflected the attention they paid to the little things. When I finally closed my first professional chapter, I knew I wanted *intention* to drive whatever I did next. To stay inspired, I decided to embrace a practice that had inspired me from afar for so long. I bought a corkboard and put "pin to paper." I've made a monthly mood board since then.

I open my old filing cabinet and retrieve nine manila envelopes, each filled with color-coordinated paper goods: family letters, museum postcards, random photos, clothing tags, thank-you notes, pretty paper, business cards, catalog pages, and magazine editorials. After laying out my inventory, I begin assembling the materials at a station under the window in my dining room. On sunny days, light streaks in, casting shadows on certain parts of the board, and these natural spotlights tangibly mark time in a way that digital creating can't. Throughout this process, I also return to my body: I move more slowly, reaching and stretching as I pin images.

There's no rhyme or reason as to what goes on the board every month, but somehow, snippets of my professional endeavors—brand logos, business cards, written tasks—always end up dead center, which poses an ongoing challenge: Can I create something worthwhile separate from the professional part of me? If I take away my work, what will endure? What *should* endure?

When one of my grandmother's infamous care packages arrived, its contents brought these questions to the forefront of my mind. Inside, an overflowing blue binder served as a handmade diary of sorts; each hole-punched paper featured intimate entries, human-interest clippings, sketches, and old letters. My grandmother had always felt she could trust me with these sorts of things—the less palatable parts of her life. I called to thank her for putting it together, and she told me there was no pressure to read it immediately. "In fact, don't look at it for another ten years," she cautioned. "Put it away."

I nodded as though she could see me and then wondered: *Why now? Where should I keep this, then?* I placed the binder in the drawer where my other memories live, reasoning that just because these things aren't in front of me doesn't mean they no longer exist. Just because they weren't with me from the start doesn't mean they were never meant to be part of my story.

Later, I considered what was still dangling on my mood board: a few unsent postcards from trips to the Picasso Museum, Guggenheim, and Phoenicia Diner; crumbling papers; blank birthday cards featuring hand-drawn renderings of rabbits and fruit. Some items have been with me for years. By now, they were filled with several pin-sized holes but were no less whole than when they came into my life. No less part of the life I had lived. I wondered what I had to prove by keeping these things tacked in the same place. Why was I holding on to things that were meant to be let go of?

I realized that, by carving out time to mood board, I consciously step back and survey the little things I've collected and kept—with their worn edges and words of affirmation—and I'm reminded of what it means to take stock of my experiences, no matter how ephemeral. My living archive is bursting at the seams, but the excess no longer tells me to achieve, make, or become something worth pinning. It's simply asking me to slow down and take hold of pieces of my story—and then, when I'm ready, to tear it down and imagine it anew.

Make a Mood Board

Make time to reflect by making a mood board of items that represent your story. Follow this week's prompts as you assemble your board.

MONDAY: Gather a collection of paper ephemera—bookmarks, notecards, and so on—that you've kept over the years. Decide what's worth holding on to and what will visually inspire you.

TUESDAY: Sort and organize your items by color, category, or texture so they are easy to find as you assemble the board.

WEDNESDAY: Before making your mood board, consider what you want it to do or evoke. Is it for professional motivation or personal reflection?

THURSDAY: Build the board, corner by corner, until the whole surface is filled.

FRIDAY: After some time away from the board, return to it and see if any more spaces need to be filled or changed.

SATURDAY: Once the board is complete, place it somewhere in view that will best serve your goals. (For example, if what you've made is career-related, place it near your desk.)

SUNDAY: Rest and read the next story.

FALL

On Leaving

I never realized how much I needed seasons until people I loved ended up in places without them. Cloudless beaches, year-round mild temperatures—lovely, but not for me. Give me clear markers of time passing.

Fall is the only season I am eager to *wait* for, and there are subtle hints of transformation all around. Usually, I hear them first. Boisterous summer laughter dies down; in its place, the soft patter of rain, the murmur of shoes meeting damp earth. Trees grow quieter, too. Only when I've recognized the low whistle of the wind do I notice how nature's leafy greens and cobalt blues have softened.

Next comes a feast for the eyes. The autumnal color palette activates my taste palate: berry and honey, chocolate and cider—these rich hues make me want to take a bite of the world. I watch leaves overtake branches, a kaleidoscope of color against an overcast sky. They sweep through the neighborhood, blanketing park benches, slate-gray sidewalks, and the steps of my building. Piles of leaves amass anywhere and everywhere. This seasonal abundance never lasts for long: Leaves begin to crumble under the weight of our lives with every step.

Maybe it's as simple as seeing kids head back to school or the change in scenery, but during fall more than any other season, I anticipate what I will leave (not lose—it's more intentional than that) and how I will grow. Summer is a fever dream, a loud hello. Fall is leaves—leaving. Its shedding is a stop sign: Bundle up, take a deep breath, and prepare for the barren aftermath of winter.

In the crisp morning hours of November, noses and ears are as red as the last dangling leaves. Soon, rows and rows of golden trees will become eclipsed by the holiday glow. But first, my birthday will arrive. This year, I'm on the cusp of a new decade.

It's been raining a lot here. Remnants of muddy brown leaves have started to sink into the carpeted stairs leading up to our apartment. The light is flatter, with fewer shadows and places to hide. I glimpse my reflection in the glass pane on our front door whenever I get home. *There you are again—shedding and growing all over. Who are you? What is going to change?*

A past me would have had the answer already—would have planned meticulously, running toward the end goal, rushing past any lingering doubts in pursuit of finding answers and becoming the person I was supposed (or taught or told or encouraged or pressured or forced) to inhabit. But I've started to greet these thresholds in calmer ways. Now, deep-purple bags hang under my eyes. I raise my eyebrows playfully, and worry lines crease on my forehead. These features make it hard to recognize the girls and women I used to be: Some have pulled away, and others I have cast off by choice. Every year, fall departs, and with it, a little piece of me joins. Grows.

What is going to change?

There is no sure answer. There is only letting the leaves fall, the dust settle, and the days unfold.

○ ◑ ●

I love seasons and their capacity to hold space for so many things at once: sweat and frost, infancy and experience, beauty and breakage, love and pain, fast and slow, gathering and parting. Still, we claw at consistency, dig our heels into the mud, grasp the things we love: *Don't leave.* But how often do we consider the departures in our lives as something to celebrate? Aren't we lucky to have a catalog of past moments showing how much we've lived?

When I can't recall the specificity of the places and people I've left, shame and grief wrap themselves around me like an old sweater. Slowly, I've become warmed by this sadness; it reminds me of my humanity. It reminds me to give them a call, send them a letter, write them a story. To look up, look down, look within. The terrain shifts and you may not remember the minute details, but you will redis-cover that there are seasons for everything: We leave and are left. We don't always get to say goodbye. When we're lucky enough to get the chance, sometimes words are not enough. But it turns out I'm good at goodbyes. I believe in them wholeheartedly. In a goodbye, there is suddenly a void—a barren aftermath—and inside it, a choice in how and where to go next.

I've learned to count goodbyes in slow seconds. Every gust of wind, every plump raindrop, every friendly nod from a stranger, every leaf crumbling beneath the weight of our stories leads us away from life as we knew it. I wrap my arms around my body to remind myself to hold on tight because the person underneath the layers will change. I now know to let myself linger in someone else's arms, too.

Fall pads the ground with beauty as we fall into new chapters. When the last of the foliage finally disappears, I stop and survey the landscape. The trees are almost naked as I stand clothed in questions. And with every ending, I'm reminded that past selves fall away. People turn over a new leaf. When they're near, I pick them up—hold them close. Then, I let them go and wait to see what comes back.

Curate a Time Capsule

Seasons come and go. Honor the moments that make them whole by curating a time capsule of things to leave for now and to revisit next season. Using the prompts below, gather items that pay homage to pivotal endings.

MONDAY: Leave a diary entry or personal note that you're ready to let go of for now.

TUESDAY: Leave something from the elements— a colorful leaf or dried flower—that signifies the season you're leaving behind.

WEDNESDAY: Leave a paper item from a recent outing—a receipt from a memorable date or a bookmark from your favorite store.

THURSDAY: Leave a travel item—a postcard or trinket— from the last place you visited.

FRIDAY: Leave a gift—or part of one—from the last person who told you goodbye.

SATURDAY: Leave a note to yourself about the things you left behind. Reflect on the decision or circum- stances that led to these departures. End the note with a question you want to answer by the time you revisit this time capsule next season.

SUNDAY: Leave time for yourself. Rest and read the next story.

IN GOOD
TIME

On Joy

I'm restless, trying to wrestle my way out of the past. I'm writing these notes standing up and thinking about what it means to move on. I've always been encouraged to walk toward opportunity. Only after crossing a recent threshold did I recognize that my strides toward "success" have often stripped me of my humanity.

I couldn't have arrived at this moment without the experience of slowing. Without watching people come and go and learning the lessons held in their shadows. Without writing it down once and then saying it over and over again: I'm not a success story—I'm a slow story through and through.

When I slow down to examine my life, I remember there is always another path forward. I'll get where I'm going, all in good time. I won't always wear a smile on the way there, but I'll carry joy in my pocket: something small enough to be lost and eventually found again but heavy enough to ground me in the moment when I feel the weight of an uncertain end. Just before a memory takes its place.

Just Practice Joy

Joy comes into our lives in myriad ways. Think about how you can practice, create, or invite joy into your week with the following prompts.

MONDAY: Just write about joy. Note the details that unexpectedly bring you happiness.

TUESDAY: Just think about joy. Reflect on the moments, people, or places that have elicited the sensation.

WEDNESDAY: Just sing about joy. Belt out lyrics or hum along to a song that always lifts your spirits.

THURSDAY: Just jump for joy. Move in a way that brings you happiness—whether it's dancing, running, skipping, walking, or jumping.

FRIDAY: Just draw joy. Draw, scribble, or paint joy in a color palette or pattern that speaks to you.

SATURDAY: Just engage in joy. Play a board game or paint a picture—indulge in an activity with no end goal other than to root yourself in the present moment.

SUNDAY: Just rest and read the next story.

RACHEL FLEIT
Filmmaker

As told to Rachel Schwartzmann

Rachel Fleit is interested in capturing the entire human experience. Known for directing projects including *Introducing, Selma Blair*, which follows actress Selma Blair as she navigates her multiple sclerosis diagnosis, and *Bama Rush*, a nuanced portrait of sorority recruitment at the University of Alabama, the esteemed filmmaker has lent her artistic prowess to projects that prize honesty, a quality Rachel is familiar with intimately. Living with alopecia universalis, Rachel has been bald since she was eighteen months old. At age four, she was encouraged by a psychologist to wear a wig as a means to adjust better in school. Rachel wore it through her teenage years, but "finally took my wig off in college," she adds. "Wearing a wig kept this barrier between me and the world, and having a secret became no longer acceptable." For Rachel, time and pace each have a part to play in her story. When it comes to endings, she's learning to lean in to slowness to recharge and remain open to new chapters, personally and professionally.

"When I was finishing the film *Introducing, Selma Blair*, I was approaching forty and thought, *I should have a partner, a child*. I was heartbroken from this relationship that didn't work out how I wanted it to; I was finishing this intense movie. Like Selma going through something massive and redefining the expectations of her life, I was redefining the expectations of *my* life. What came from that ending was a huge rebirth. I started to look at myself differently once that film was sold and premiered. I began to believe that I belonged in this world of filmmaking in a way that I didn't know before.

Doubt never ends. I have impostor syndrome, fear—but I know in my heart that I belong in this world of storytellers. With that film, I was given the gift of belonging. I got the validation that I needed. I had to find the validation in myself first. Not to sound too cliché, but when I was going through this emotional upheaval, it was a real rock bottom. I had to find myself—and I did. I found a new understanding of who I am, what I want, and what I thought I wanted.

Patience is my 'God-given talent.' I'm extremely patient with everyone except myself. I have an extraordinary capacity to pay attention, listen, and create a safe space, which is 90 percent of my job in filmmaking. It's innate, and I do not think it can be learned. I think it can only be gathered.

But slowness, I don't like it! Right now, I'm really trying to find a way to take time for myself, nurse the creative hangover, and not rush into a new project if it doesn't feel 1,000 percent right. I'm trusting my gut on who I want to work with and surround myself with, personally and professionally. I'm trying to learn how to be slow—but I want the edit to happen fast. I want to see the receipts of my hard-earned patience, and I want to know the story.

I've learned a lot about myself as a filmmaker and also what I need as a person. I'm an introverted extrovert. I can be extremely effusive in a social setting and walk into a room, twirl around, and sprinkle fairy dust. Then I have to retreat. I cherish my solitude, and I need it. I'm so proud that I've gotten to a place in my adult life where I can be alone and entertain myself in my solitude. It's like patience: I don't believe you can learn it, but maybe, with experience, you can acquire skills that make you a more patient person. Solitude is very similar because it has to become a practice.

I find it extremely gratifying to complete something, but I like to leave my skin in the world. I think: *What's next?* Currently, I get a little sad from endings. I didn't allow myself the space to feel the sadness of letting that go after *Introducing, Selma Blair* premiered. I'm exploring disappointment, sadness, and grief as an engine for my next creative project. I hate to say this, but I think that sadness, grief, longing, and disappointment are the engines of my creativity.

I'm taking the time for the next one, slowing down, and not doing much. I'm spending time in reciprocal relationships and being curious. I'm keeping the channel open and seeing when projects come to me—having the faith that the right thing will come to me at the right time. There's a lot of putting trust in the proverbial universe that I'm doing right now. I think that's so important."

HEAVY

On Solitude

Solitude is heavy. It's a stack of bricks or a weighted blanket, depending on the day. Even when I put it down, the load isn't always lightened. Often, I'm still holding on to memories of deep, meaningful conversations with no concrete recollection of what was actually said, especially on my part. I'm not exactly sure what to call this—perhaps the feeling or the act of sharing outweighed the words. I think about this a lot whenever I'm alone. I remember that wholeness can be mistaken for heaviness, and silence can still be a story.

Make Solitude Your Destination

PROMPT

There's no need to travel far to rest and recharge. Make solitude your "destination" by integrating these prompts into your daily travels.

MONDAY: Start your week in solitude. Write about how you plan to harness a sense of solitude in the places you like to visit outside your home.

TUESDAY: Take a solo stroll or lunch date with a journal in tow. Write about the things you wouldn't usually talk about when in the company of others.

WEDNESDAY: Visit a nearby location—a museum, a restaurant—that best accommodates solitude and replenishment. Write about the energy in the room.

THURSDAY: Read your favorite book, story, or poem aloud to yourself. Write about how it feels to hear your voice relay ideas or words you love.

FRIDAY: Look at a piece of art or watch a film that embodies your definition of *solitude*. Write about how it calms or captures your imagination.

SATURDAY: Consider what you've mistaken for solitude in the past. Write about a definition of this idea with the experience you've garnered from following these prompts.

SUNDAY: Rest at home in solitude and read the next story.

MAKE US YOUR HOME AGAIN

On Friendship

There are your friends, and there are people you know. They are there forever, and then one day, they are gone. They give you strength or envelop you in sorrow—or maybe you do that yourself. It's harder to discern the more you become hardened by life. I know this firsthand, but I'm trying to soften. I'm trying to meet them again.

People mill out of subway stations, talking loudly on cell phones. They wear thrifted coats and expensive purses. Cigarettes or MetroCards hang from the edge of their lips. Lust and lies wait on their tongues. They love to be present without focusing on the present. For a time, you might have struggled to pick me out of this sea of sameness: New Yorkers itching to make a statement while still yearning to belong.

After years of enforced isolation, I entered the city, and it was an awkward reunion. Overwhelm bumped into me as I wove through masses of new, younger people continuing the story I—and so many others before me—had been a part of. I was downtown, and summer was around the corner. I shielded my eyes as I wandered toward a beloved restaurant I used to frequent. It was more than food that beckoned me in.

I first met the restaurant's owners—a stylish and lively husband-wife duo—within months of their opening. I quickly learned that they embraced you as their own. They became a quiet fixture in my life in the following years: They milled around the bustling background of my meetings. They participated in lifestyle interviews and projects for my clients. When I was off the clock, they brought me complimentary desserts and drinks. They winked at me as I engaged in long conversations with people I now no longer speak with. I would catch them sitting at the tables with other patrons. There was laughter and service. Their approach to people sharpened my understanding of friendship. It was enough just to be there—sitting beside someone.

The restaurant's original location had nearly tripled in size since its inception, swaths of it girls and hip professionals still stormed the tables. I was one of the few people eating alone. While I was waiting for my dish to arrive, a familiar face caught my eye, and one of the owners appeared next to me. "Rachel!" he exclaimed. "How are you? Been a long time." We elbow-bumped and exchanged a few more pleasantries. "It's good to have you in. You used to be here so much." He paused before turning away. "Make us your home again."

We had known each other in such a specific context, but the sincerity of his invitation made me sit up a little straighter. This kindness paired well with my meal. I ate hungrily and managed not to swallow the smile on my lips.

○ ◑ ●

I've never minded being alone, but for many years, I was rarely by myself. As the certified wallflower of a friend group, I was there to watch, listen, and help when I could. At every gathering, we'd take a picture: A moment was captured, and a relationship was preserved—proof that we were there and happy.

Later, while inspecting the photo, they might wonder about that stranger in the corner of the frame who marked their memory. They wouldn't immediately recognize that the stranger was their partner, collaborator, client, friend. Me. And even though we ran off the page and far away from one another, it was nobody's fault. The story changed. They changed. We changed.

Now, amid constant change, the world continues calling. I find fewer people on the other end. I think that's why my heart starts racing when I see a missed call: Here is proof that even among the chaos, someone might miss me back.

○ ◑ ●

Something primal happens when you're young: You look for your people, and suddenly you belong to them. Then life does what it does. Work, responsibilities, romance, jealousy, distraction, and change pull at the seams. Community is harder to come by.

I'm grateful to have been a part of many different communities. I was a tastemaker at lavish dinner parties, trading style tips and trend predictions. I was a fledgling founder in office buildings, making my case and making work friends. I was someone who was never meant to run a business and made it her business to begin anew. I was a writer revising her story and connecting with storytellers. I was an anxious woman in a global pandemic who had been tired for a long time and, in some ways, had been given an out. I was an absent friend who, like most of us, still aimed to be a good person.

Through it all, I've had to make promises to myself before I can extend myself to others. This essay was my first attempt in a long time: I wanted to hold all of my past and present friends on the page, to capture them not in captivity but in curiosity. I wanted to write about friends who are lovely and lonely. I wanted to write about friends who I worked with hard and fell out with harder. I wanted to write about friends who've lost control or willingly disappeared. I wanted to write *beyond* society's cultural syllabus: sepia-tinted coming-of-age portraits, stories about women arriving in the city or unraveling in the country, cinematic studies that are all vibes and no plot. The adage goes that we don't always get what we want. Instead, I remembered a conversation with a new friend (whose one screen and thousands of miles separate us but who is a kindred spirit nonetheless). We both agreed that we shouldn't cast off clichés. They exist for a reason, and we don't always have to reinvent the wheel. And maybe, even after what we've all been through and are taught to expect from one another, it's still enough to sit side by side with someone.

○ ◑ ●

Summer came and went, slowly replaced by fall's brand of warmth. I invited a few writers to my apartment for dinner ahead of the holiday season. I hadn't hosted anyone in years. They arrived one by one, setting down home-cooked meals, sugary desserts, and their own private battles. A familiar feeling of panic bloomed in my chest. There was no reason to feel this way, but I briefly excused myself anyway and took refuge in the bathroom. I watched my skin shape-shift from pale to pink, and as I waited for the palette to subside, I stared at my reflection and reflected on the people who became my friends, the friends who became people I knew, and how each of them made me the woman in the mirror.

Rooms away, the writers in attendance chatted about art and film and love. Two were old friends, and all three were bound together by a literary scene I had not yet fully embraced. All of them had experienced varying degrees of my shyness and shortcomings—but none knew I hid a bottle of water and a box of medicine in the cabinet to stave off anxiety whenever someone came to the house. They didn't know how I longed to know them beyond the pages of the books they wrote. They hadn't known me long enough to understand how much their presence brought me hope. It was too soon to disclose any of that information, but it wasn't too soon to write another ending to the night.

As sounds of muffled laughter and the chime of dinnerware permeated the space, I thought about how sometimes, when I'm lonely, I'll pull a book I've already read off the shelf. I'll flip through its pages, and as the words balloon into full-blown narratives, I'll recall the moments that made me smile, giggle, or cry. To me, this is the embodiment of friendship: holding something dear, knowing it inside out—a beginning, middle, and ending right there in the palm of your hand. In many ways, friendship is the truest slow story. It transcends genre and form. It's fact pinning fiction to the wall. It's promising never to turn away, even when we're far away off the page, in another place entirely.

Eventually, I opened the door to my dining room. Their faces brightened, and the restaurateur's invitation came flooding back: *Make us your home again.* Those words became a calling as I watched new friends gather around the table in my home. I sat by their side. I let myself be carried by their voices.

Write about Friendship

PROMPT

What would happen if we continually reimagined what friendship could be? Consider these prompts as you write your way
through a new week.

MONDAY: Write about an unexpected ending in a friendship and how it affected you both.

TUESDAY: Write about the friends that taught you what
endings could look like.

WEDNESDAY: Write an alternate ending for your favorite
book, film, or poem about friendship.

THURSDAY: Write about the questions you want to ask
at each phase of a new friendship.

FRIDAY: Write a new answer to a question an old friend
of yours often asks.

SATURDAY: Write the ending of your greatest
friendship-love story—then write a new beginning.

SUNDAY: Rest and read the next story.

REMINDERS

On Slowing Down, Logging Off, and Creating Consciously

"A specific activity that can help with creating consciously is to think or write about your ideal life—what does this look like to you? From there, think about your intentions and goals and write a list. Reflect on how you're living your life and identifying how much this list aligns with what you're currently doing. Having the awareness to recognize our strengths and areas for growth—while also working on accepting that we are human and not perfect—is very important in this process."

LIZ BEECROFT, LCSW
Psychotherapist and Founder of MENTL.SESH

"Notice what makes you feel alive and energized. When I spend time meditating, dancing, in nature, and doing practices that connect me to a good state, then I can feel the contrast noticeably if I spend too much time on screens, working, or creating mindlessly. Learning to listen to our bodies communicate with us is worthwhile. To build a stronger relationship with my body, I do things that bring me that feeling of aliveness first thing in the morning before I can mentally rationalize an excuse. This way, finding my way back to well-being later in the day, after responding to emails or completing whatever essential work there is, is much easier."

ANISA BENITEZ
Actor and Artist

"Before we can move slowly and consciously, we must realize we have been moving too quickly, missing things—missing life. This, for me, is the great challenge. When I find I am focused on the *end* rather than the *process*, that is a sign for me to be curious about what I might be rushing toward or, more often, avoiding. Why am I running faster than I want to run, to finish this workout as soon as possible, rather than enjoying the feeling of running? Why am I listening to this audiobook at 1.75 speed? Why am I skipping pages in the bedtime stories for my daughter? I have to remember I don't want to rush each step of my day because this is rushing through my life, rushing toward my own death. If I am curious about why I am moving in this way, rather than shaming myself for it, I am better able to understand what's really happening and slow my energy. Often, I'm moving fast in an attempt to outrun anxiety of some sort. I try to say to myself: 'It's okay if you don't read all the books, write a thousand perfect words a day, and accomplish everything on the list in one afternoon.' I stop running and walk when I feel like it. I slow my audiobook to 1.0 speed or wash the dishes in silence. I read all the pages in the bedtime story. And when I move this way, these moments become the best parts of my day and, by extension, my life."

ANNA HOGELAND
Author of *The Long Answer*

"Over the past year, I replaced my house's liquid hand soap dispensers with bars of high-quality bar soap. The transition to bar soap was an environmental and aesthetic move. What I didn't know was that I was inadvertently engineering a tool for slow living. I was already familiar with bar soaps from my childhood and felt a familiarity with the bar of soap's weight in my hand and the charm of its cozy soap dish on the sink. Rolling a bar of soap in my hands feels like slow living because it connects me to my body: I am actually *holding* the soap. There is no plastic-vessel middleman. The running water and the rolling of the hands in one another is a sort of beautiful tea ceremony—one that is episodically built into the day. It slows me down every time."

OLIVIA JOFFREY
Founder of Olivia Joffrey Studio

"As a creative, it can be hard to 'turn off'—there's a sort of low hum of energy that compels me to keep scrolling and searching for content. But ironically, it's when I do slow down that I start to notice the things around me and really *see* them. Sometimes I have to force myself to get into that zone. I'll challenge myself to pick a color and document every time I see that color in a day. Or I'll take a drive and look for good typography references in old signage. Whatever it is, the process of looking with purpose is sort of like a visual meditation—it forces me to stay in the moment and focus my brain. If you're ever feeling creatively spread thin, or you just need a bit of a break, give some sort of thematic scavenger hunt a try."

ALI LABELLE
Creative Director

"The thing that consistently reminds me to slow down is the inherent physicality of my work. If I want to end up with a piece I'm proud of, I can't rush. Saying yes to too many projects and setting unrealistic deadlines are surefire ways for me to hurry and lose focus. But when I'm moving at a comfortable and measured pace, making things with my hands is a grounding escape. As someone who skews anxious, this type of practice is invaluable for my state of mind. The more present I am for the work, the better the final result. If I move too quickly, there's not enough heart in it, and it shows—there's less room for finessing details and making little last-minute tweaks. While these finer points may not be visible to an outsider's eye, mine is immediately drawn to them. Getting the right amount of wonky whimsicality on a candelabra, mixing the paint color for a bow candleholder, and making the perfect swirl of frosting on a cake clock: These tasks keep me in the moment and are worth slowing down for."

ANAMARIA MORRIS
Creator of All Kinds

"Don't condition yourself to a story that it will be 'hard' to log off, that 'I'm so busy I have to work all weekend.' This is a way we condition the mind to be addicted to productivity, emails, or checking off items on the endless to-do list. Instead of making it a struggle or telling yourself a story, decide to make it easy. Consciously log off on Sundays (or for longer) and be 100 percent in the present moment without guilt. We think that productivity begets more productivity—it does not! We need space. We need time away from social media. We need time to be with our thoughts. We need time to meditate and breathe. We need time to integrate. We need time to check in with ourselves. This spaciousness is something we must prioritize. Whether you can only get five minutes in the morning or a full hour or a full day—take it and make it yours."

TONYA PAPANIKOLOV
Founder of Rainbo, Holistic Nutritionist, and Health Educator

"Sometimes the best ideas come from doing nothing, being outside, talking to people, or while on a nice walk by yourself. When you're feeling stuck, leave your phone at home. Go to nature—or even just for a walk around the block. Speak to someone on the street, and you'll be recharged with fresh energy and creative superpowers. When you travel, enjoy the journey. Look up to the sky, and you'll see so many things you usually miss when your mind is somewhere else."

NATALIA SWARZ
Founder of Hôtel Weekend

LEAH THOMAS

Activist, Author, and Founder
of Intersectional Environmentalist

As told to Rachel Schwartzmann

Leah Thomas, founder of the climate justice collective Intersectional Environmentalist, experienced an
explosive—and "confusing"—period of professional
growth. Following the social justice movements of
2020, Leah arrived at a turning point. "After I was able
to lay a foundation, I started focusing on changing up
the pacing," she says. "I spent three months completely
single, not working on any projects or doing too much
writing, just resting." While certain chapters came to
a close during that time, Leah contends that endings
themselves are never finite. "The pace can change,
and I'm just trying to listen and be a little bit more
intentional."

"Endings are a transference into something else. I embrace that because many of my big career or relationship moments that ended or came to a close were just due to listening to my intuition. My mind and heart told me that a shift needed to occur. Endings can feel a bit scary at times. I don't want to call an ending a conclusion but rather a pivot in another direction that feels more aligned.

I have anxiety. Anxiety is often portrayed in the media as cute and quirky, but there are a lot of non-quirky-and-cute parts of having it. As I've gotten older—and now that I'm at a place where I have coping skills—I want to be in control of things less. In other periods of my life when I was really anxious, endings were so scary. A lot of anxiety is catastrophizing when you don't know the outcome. Maybe one of those possibilities is an end.

A lot of the endings in my life have led to my greatest accomplishments. I guess with that anticipatory anxiety of thinking, *If this happens, what's going to happen in my life?* and having so many of those moments, being able to feel that process of heartbreak come to an end or transfer into something else—empowerment, a rest period, or another project—is such a cool feeling. Endings have been the best teachers, and a lot of those endings also have to do with failure. Endings are something I definitely welcome a lot more and am less afraid of now.

I would tell people there's another side to an ending. It's a process, just like grief. It's a circle. It's not linear. There's that transference, and your emotions will evolve throughout the process. The beginning can be clouded by a lot of anticipation. Then with some endings, there's no anticipation, it just happens, and it's entirely out of your control. That feels even scarier sometimes. But trust that your emotions will go on a journey, that there's another side of it, and that you will be okay."

TIMESTAMPS

On Choices

00:00 My emails are categorized into folders that have pre-made titles like "Primary" and "Updates." I didn't choose this setup, but I've also never done anything about it.

1:00 As I wade through my inbox now, I realize most of what's there I never asked for in the first place.

2:00 Someone tells me we spend so much of our lives saying no to ourselves.

3:00 There are days when I would like to say no more than *know* more.

4:00 *No*, I don't want to shop now. *No*, I don't want to set up a quick call. *No*, I don't want to join the waitlist.

5:00 Because on the other side of *no* are long-game lessons: quiet, emptiness, outrage, slowness, renewal, space.

6:00 What can you do with all that time?

7:00 You can rename folders and reclaim your life.

8:00 You can unsubscribe from your habits the same way you'd unsubscribe from a newsletter.

9:00 You can think carefully about what to say to someone waiting on your words.

10:00 You can forgive yourself for taking too long.

11:00 You can forget to send a response altogether.

12:00 You can care about someone even without saying a word: check the forecast in the place they live, send a meme or a prayer, donate to a cause they care about in their name.

13:00 You can care about yourself through small gestures— like enjoying a glass of water in a fancy cup or letting your eyes wander away from the screen and toward the sky.

14:00 You can express your gratitude without ever opening your mouth—a smile, a hug, or a wink will do.

15:00 You can mourn what's been lost every time you've lost a battle—and then let it go.

16:00 You can talk about something everyone's heard before. (They've never heard it said at *this* moment, after all.)

17:00 You can enjoy the silences rarely found in a world sustained by screams.

18:00 You can say no to yourself and then ask yourself why.

19:00 You can ask yourself why and then say no.

20:00 You can admit, "No, I don't know," to a question that's asked.

21:00 You can tell a story without ever picking up a pen.

22:00 You can write a new ending while still honoring your beginning.

23:00 You can accept that you can't control anything, but you can choose to do anything—or at least try. The question is: Will you?

Celebrate Your Choices

Slow down and celebrate your strides—and the decisions you've made along the way. Reflect on pivotal choices and chapters in your life with the following prompts in mind.

MONDAY: Write about a choice you made that unexpectedly changed your life.

TUESDAY: Write about a choice that was made for you and how it changed the way you see yourself.

WEDNESDAY: Write about a choice that brought you joy.

THURSDAY: Write about a choice that you helped someone else make.

FRIDAY: Write about a person you chose and how they've nourished your life.

SATURDAY: Write about a choice you'll have to make in the future and how you'll take what you've learned from past decisions into account.

SUNDAY: Choose to rest and read the next story.

THE OTHER SEASON

On Stillness

The other season lives alone. She moved away from Mother Earth's grasp so she wouldn't have to keep up with the pace of modern life. Call her a feeling or a pause or a plan, or nothing at all: She's pretty unpredictable in that way.

The other season moves between soil and sky, alerting us to little things, sometimes stopping us in our tracks altogether. Often, she gets confused with boredom or stagnancy, but the other season moves us in ways we never imagined.

A few years ago, the other season appeared on my doorstep as winter left and spring unpacked. She hadn't spoken to either in a while, and I hadn't spoken to her in much longer. We were due for a visit. Then disaster struck around the globe, and the other season stuck around longer than either of us anticipated. When life returned to its usual rhythms, I found that the other season still lingered in the air, which was surprising, given her quiet nature.

Many people had no use for the other season in a world with lush Aprils and brisk Novembers. They especially want to forget her now. But I came around to her presence and learned that the other season is tough. She's not interested in comforting or burdening. She doesn't adhere to traditional calendars or clocks. The other season goes by her name for a reason: *Other* indicates a separation. She can't conform because she has no clear shape. She moves slowly and deliberately until we're forced to see the other season for what she is: another way of being.

Stillness as a season.

The other season storms through the digital world, too— it's her least favorite place. But this landscape has the perfect conditions to stifle us into a stillness we don't always recognize. We succumb to paralysis, which masks itself as rest, and the other season sighs. We feel her breath on our necks. A shiver runs through our spines, and we can't place the feeling. *Are you slowing down or just stunted? Can you sit in stillness instead of running—scrolling—away from it? What will you learn if you still yourself rather than steel yourself against everything?* The other season is listening when you ask these questions—just know that her answer will always remain the same: "It doesn't matter why or how or where. I'm here. Don't turn away from me this time."

○ ◑ ●

Create a Calendar

What would happen if you created a new calendar dedicated to the other season(s) in your life? Follow this week's prompts for guidance.

MONDAY: Name your other season—think: *stillness, happiness, adventure*—and write about its attributes so you know what to look for when (or if) it arrives.

TUESDAY: Decide how you'll measure time in your other season. Will it be in seconds or smiles? Days or weather?

WEDNESDAY: Similar to other seasonal pastimes (like fall foliage hunting or summer beach days), write about the rituals you'd like to associate with your other season.

THURSDAY: Give your other season "holidays" or check-points. Write about their meanings and how you need to celebrate.

FRIDAY: Reflect on whether you'll share about this season with those in your life or keep it to yourself. Write about what you'd like to see in both scenarios.

SATURDAY: Create artwork to accompany your calendar page. Think about symbols or colors that best represent your other season's mood or intention.

SUNDAY: Store your calendar somewhere meaningful, and refer to it when you feel restless or uncertain. In the meantime, rest and read the next story.

NEIGHBORHOOD STORY

On Quiet

I was waiting to place an order at my go-to café when a little boy locked eyes with me. He shuffled over and then froze when he realized I wasn't the person he was looking for. I heard a woman a few paces ahead saying, "She looks like Mama, but that's not Mama!" He wandered toward me a few more times until his actual mother appeared. The two adults smiled at me briefly as he bolted in their direction. And that was it—the game was over. The line kept moving, though I couldn't shake the feeling that this moment was supposed to show me something.

This interaction occurred at the height of a period when I found it impossible to leave my neighborhood. I was tired—in a way that a self-care Sunday or a vacation couldn't fix—and needed to contain my exhaustion within a few-block radius. This also meant I was lacking in "big" experiences.

Often, I didn't see or say much to anyone (though I don't think that's the same as not wanting to know them).

I've always been a quiet person, and living in New York has only underscored how much of my character directly opposes its energy. And yet, quiet is more than an identifying characteristic—it's an experience that's happened to me, and in some cases, because of me. Locale aside, quiet has remained a constant, though only in recent years have I started to understand it not as an advantage or a hindrance but as a fact of who I am and what I'm drawn to.

I don't always have to say much to have a story worth telling. Ultimately, we all want to be happy, and the stories that get us there are often without consequence to anyone but ourselves. That's why, when I bumped into an old acquaintance a few weeks later, I was surprised at how moved I was to see her. By then, she had become a relatively famous television personality. Ever the adept speaker—her voice smooth like honey—I listened more than I responded even as she asked me questions. Most of our chitchat focused on the very street we were standing on. "Don't ever move!" she exclaimed after gushing about the calm pace of the neighborhood. A swirl of sirens and passersby encroached on the moment, so I only smiled before we went our separate ways. Later, I mentioned to my husband that she was the first person I had hugged in months who wasn't immediate family—and I realized that quiet had taught me to make meaning out of any experience. I could feel at peace with my choice to be out in the world, barely saying a word but greeting it just the same.

Enjoy Quality Quiet Time

Quiet can take on new shapes depending on the context. Rediscover—and embrace—quality quiet time in your personal, professional, or creative settings by keeping these prompts in mind.

MONDAY: Focus on a quiet thought. Write about how this idea or image quiets your mind.

TUESDAY: Remember a quiet moment that moved you—this can be a scene from a movie or something that unfolded in front of you in real time. Write about how it feels to revisit the experience from afar.

WEDNESDAY: Create a quiet playlist. Reflect on why these songs, podcasts, or audiobooks quiet your environment.

THURSDAY: Question quiet. What does quiet mean to you and your community?

FRIDAY: Define *quiet*. Write an expanded definition of the term that considers your goals for living a slower life.

SATURDAY: Share quiet. Invite a friend or loved one for a quiet activity—whether it's reading in the park or attending a film. Reflect on how it feels to be in the company of someone without the expectation to speak.

SUNDAY: Embrace quiet alone. Rest quietly and read the next story.

JEZZ CHUNG

Multidisciplinary Artist and Public Speaker

As told to Rachel Schwartzmann

Jezz Chung describes themself as someone who infuses possibility into their work. Even as a self-proclaimed dreamer, Jezz firmly believes in action. After designing their dream job in advertising, which focused on building equity through creativity and well-being, the pandemic and subsequent social justice movements stirred something inside Jezz. They couldn't shake the growing dissonance between their current job and a deeper calling from within—so they made a change. Ending one career to pursue many passions has led them to discover a healthier pace with storytelling and community building. As Jezz puts it: "Slowness is still a speed."

"Before I realized I was neurodivergent, I thought I was slower than everyone. I thought there was something wrong with the pace that I needed. I blamed myself. I made myself the problem before realizing I'm *not* the problem. It's the systems and the pacing that is demanded. It's the neuro-norm pace, expectations, and environment. I love that I move at the pace that I do. I love that I'm intentional. I love that I need space to process and integrate things. The neurodiversity paradigm, which I study a lot, frees us to think about how everyone's brain is different. Everyone processes things differently, and there's nothing wrong with that.

Another huge part of making that change in my life was that my body was sending me very clear cues that this pace wasn't working for me. That showed up in many depressive spells where I wasn't functioning for days. It was tough to do the smallest things, like get out of bed, brush my teeth, shower, and have daily conversations. My nervous system was so fried and activated, and I needed to soothe it. I needed to somatically locate where that discomfort was and what that was pointing me to. I thought of it as changing the shape of my life to change the shape of my body, so this new life I was designing for myself could hold this new shape of me— and the shape of the world I want to see, too.

For a long time, I didn't think living as an actor, speaker, and writer was possible. I thought I had to pursue a career that was more practical and more 'stable.' It took a lot of personal change and transformation to realize that it's more dangerous for me not to listen to myself and not to pursue my dreams of writing books, acting in shows and films, and speaking to people about my story. My body is so much more content living in the truth of my calling than fitting myself into the standards or expectations prescribed to me.

When we feel that pressure or urge to push ourselves or perform productivity, it's important to ask ourselves where that voice comes from. Once we recognize that that voice usually comes from forces outside of us— instead of our inner world—then I think it's easier to redirect that voice and to move from a sense of security, clarity, and confidence. The pace we need is okay and necessary for the world we need to create. *What do I need? What is needed?* Those are questions we just don't ask enough. But those are questions I'm always asking myself to help guide me and move my life in a direction that centers care and community and helps us build a more sustainable, inclusive, and equitable world."

GOLDEN HOUR

On Light

If we don't have light, then we don't have a story. Light marks time: However quietly, it sweeps through our rooms one day and hides from us the next. I'm writing this at a point when light will glisten for just a few hours a day. While it's still bright outside, it feels right to tell you about what I can see: gas lamps flickering in the distance, neighbors milling in and out of brownstones and businesses, a jovial guy walking a dog on the ledge of the stone wall encircling the park entrance— the pup trotting gleefully ahead like a tightrope walker at the circus. This city *is* a circus these days, with lovers, drifters, and artists roaming the streets and blotting the sidewalks with their dreams. It's a place devoid of consistency but filled with constant movement. All the while, golden hour slowly descends, adding texture and tempo to these vibrant scenes. Light marks time and people. No matter where you are when the day is nearing its end, when you no longer have the energy to reach out to people, reach out and let yourself be touched by the hazy yellow curtain that blankets the earth before the sun sets. Golden hour makes you look and makes it easier to put one foot in front of the other. I love the way it changes throughout the year. The quiet winter sky is made brighter with rivulets of orange light that give way to cotton-candy clouds. Golden hour in the summer gives a whole new meaning to warmth: Its palette swivels out, revealing streaks of citrus, hibiscus, honey, and mustard. But no matter the season, those pools of light eventually fade into dusk. The sun goes down, and so do my blinds. Then I'm cloistered in the only place that feels like home. So few places in the world give us that reassurance. So few sensations—like light—show us how much we carry. I wish we trusted ourselves and our strength more. Light marks time and space. I'm breathless now. I've read this aloud—I'm always so quiet—and I need to feel the words coming into being. The world doesn't give much space for breaks, paragraphs or otherwise, but I'm learning to pause, even when it feels like a race against the clock. The light is running out, and I'm chasing after it. The words are tumbling out, and I'm getting ahead of myself. It's the deep breaths after no breaks and fast sprints that are slow. And with each exhale, I'm creating light between the dark spaces. When the day nears its end, loved ones remind us we'll find our way through the darkness. If we don't have light, then we won't see our way to the end of the tunnel. So give me golden hour, and I'll give you my trust. Because if we don't have trust, then we don't stand a chance.

Go Out at Golden Hour

Shine a light on the ordinary parts of your life by walking during golden hour, the hour before sunset. Watch, document, and reflect on your surroundings with the following prompts in mind.

MONDAY: Photograph a scene in the same spot each day this week during golden hour. Write about how the environment changes as the week progresses.

TUESDAY: Follow your shadow. Photograph or sketch different shadows as the hour passes.

WEDNESDAY: Look for light. Record a video of how light shifts across the tops of buildings, streets, or trees.

THURSDAY: Document how the colors change as the hour passes. When you get home, create a golden-hour color palette through art, fashion, food, or whatever medium feels right to you.

FRIDAY: Write about how golden hour makes you feel. When you get home, crowdsource a playlist or reading recommendation list based on this mood.

SATURDAY: Write about time. How has golden hour shifted your perception of time after completing these exercises?

SUNDAY: Slow down at sunset. Rest and read the next story.

SHELL

On Trust

When I was in high school, I became "Snail." I doodled snails
on anyone and everything, and the finished product was
never very good. The antennas looked more like cat ears; each
face was adorned with a small smile and two small dots for
eyes. I'm not sure where the ritual began, though the scene
usually looked like this: The room thrummed with energy
only found before the teacher's arrival; a classmate slammed
their wrist on my desk while craning to talk to someone
across the way or sneaking a text. Then I quickly got to work
imprinting what became my signature emblem. I was a shy,
dreamy teenager, so I suppose this made sense to my peers.
A few people even thought "Snail" was my last name.

I drew on myself, too: intricate floral and line arrangements
up and down my calves and wrists. I preferred art-store markers over ballpoint pens as I attempted to mimic the tattoos
I saw on the (presumably college) kids around Astor Place.

The snail, however, was mainly reserved for others. Because of my dedication to the craft, it became an exchange—take birthday and holiday cards, for instance: "I tried to draw it just for you," one card reads above a surprisingly realistic rendering of the shelled creature. (I was always grateful for these notes and have saved every single one.)

I don't know why it was a snail. I have no resonant memories of them as a child. Perhaps I was drawn to a creature with built-in protection, privacy. The inherent slowness. Those things feel so rare for us humans.

It's ironic, given that pacing myself never factored into being young, especially in New York. Here, urgency is the elixir of youth, and naivete is a close second. Here, I charged toward all opportunities. I was ambitious and hardworking, but a steady drip of fear coursed through my veins, too. I was in the best place to begin a life, except I didn't want to grow up.

I masked my fear with sensitivity and thoughtfulness, which got mistaken for maturity. It was true, to an extent: I had lived through losses and unstable landscapes in a way that some of my peers hadn't. In other ways, I was a highly sheltered girl. That dual state of holding on to my child-at-heart attitude while having a firm grip on the future often left me feeling paralyzed. I was an ordinary person with no shell to retreat into, so I marked others with the closest thing to that symbol of protection I could think of, initiating a bond between us.

Sometimes my mind tricks itself into thinking I knew myself better as a teenager than I do now. Then I'll leaf through

an old journal or recall a conversation from that time and
realize I really didn't know a thing. Upon further reflection,
it seems it was more of a matter of trust than knowing. When
we're young, the structures we're told to trust in—academia,
real estate, cities—can challenge our sense of self in quiet
ways, because we haven't yet gained the experience to know
otherwise. Still, we often trust ourselves in youth more than
we realize, even when it feels impossible to emerge from our
respective shells.

And while we aren't always given reasons to trust *each other*,
when we make the decision to, we live a little more fully.
We choose to decide how we show up for people. Those
decisions have ripple effects. The effects sharpen our instincts.
Instincts tell us our stories.

In my case, the snail was both my foreground and fore-
shadowing. It was a symbolic guide that said: *I know you
think you need to go fast—and maybe right now you do.
You can also trust that certain things are meant to come full
circle, even those unassuming sketches on your friends' hands.
Your small work of art might just become the work of your life.*

Draw Yourself

PROMPT

Art is a mode of self-expression, and it can also inspire a form of trust if we pay close enough attention to ourselves and the things that make up our world. This week, draw a series of self-portraits with the following prompts in mind.

MONDAY: Draw your reflection. Caption the image with one thing you trust most about yourself.

TUESDAY: Draw yourself in a series of shapes. Caption the image with a few sentences about how you've learned to trust yourself in abstract or unclear situations.

WEDNESDAY: Draw yourself as the animal that best represents who you are. Caption the image with a phrase that inspires trust.

THURSDAY: Draw yourself in the future. Caption the image with a few sentences about trust and time.

FRIDAY: Draw yourself at an ending. Caption the image with a few sentences about why you trusted yourself in this chapter in your life.

SATURDAY: Draw your reflection. Caption the image with what you've learned about trust as you've gone through these exercises.

SUNDAY: Reflect on this week's artworks, viewing your drawings side by side. Then rest and read the next story.

THE WORLD IS
FULL OF YES

On Hope

My father's faith in me is as strong as his father's disinterest was in him. I'm allowed to say this because it's true—we've discussed it at length. Somehow, we as a society still don't talk enough about fathers and how their hearts break, too. My father's heart has been broken for a long time, but he's made something out of the pain. I know this because I'm like him in so many ways.

Like the season he was born into, my father is made of transitions and prone to contradictions: bright and calm, cold and gloomy. These conditions also set the tone for his upbringing.

His father, my grandfather, immigrated from Ukraine to the United States in 1926. He fought in World War II and was awarded a Purple Heart medal. He eventually became a high school teacher. My grandmother grew up in a tar-paper house with a detached outhouse in the Pacific Northwest and married her former English teacher—my grandfather, seventeen years her senior. My grandmother made art, and my grandfather favored the art of living well. They raised two children in Oakland, California.

My father was a relatively well-adjusted kid, but his home life was difficult. He was never quite able to meet my grandfather's expectations (or ego). He struggled to live peacefully with my grandmother, who didn't find sobriety until he was grown. He and his sister operated on separate levels entirely.

After high school, my father went on to study acting at a renowned dramatic arts academy in Los Angeles. He didn't book many jobs, but he did meet my mother. "Would you like a drink?" my father drunkenly asked her at a party. Later, they recognized each other standing in line for the bathroom, and their story continued.

As a couple, they waited tables and partied hard. They lived in a beautiful apartment in Pasadena only to discover the trees outside of their window had become home to an infestation of rats. My mother wasn't asked back to the academy. My father wasn't sure an actor's life suited him. For every step forward, there seemed to be subtle signs of looming troubles. But they made it work for a while.

My parents married in 1986 and separated a little over two decades later. Within that period, a slew of experiences unfolded before them: I was born in San Francisco in 1992, marking my parents' evolution from aspiring artists to couple to family. Together, we moved throughout the region, then to two other states. The world was our stage, and in some way, my parents' theatrics never ceased: I looked to my mother for drama and romance, and my father for dark comedy. I was trying to come of age behind the scenes.

When we arrived in New York from Texas, my father's life began on a different stage—one with poles and parties. Gone were the days of sterile office cubicles or dusty stockrooms. Now, he was a gentleman in a club that was sustained on reverie and debauchery. Five nights a week, he cashiered or managed in an environment outside my realm of knowledge. After each shift, he emerged when the city that never sleeps finally nodded off (because everyone deserves to close their eyes for a little while).

The problem is that *he* never closed his eyes. He carried himself through an unconventional career change. He carried the family through moves, my mother's health crises, and the usual weights of marriage and parenthood. But a person can only take so much. As a teenager, I realized he had hit his limit. For as silly and lighthearted as he could be, his twin self became a defining presence: He shook with rage and retreated to the computer. His bloodshot eyes and tense gaze chilled the room. At our lowest points, I was afraid of him and for him.

I was a sophomore in high school when my parents finally called it quits. At first, he moved into our rental house's basement to remain close to me. Sometimes I'd hear the faint sound of video-game explosions or catch a whiff of freshly brewed coffee wafting up into the kitchen. He continued to work nights, but by day, we slowly rekindled a bond that had fluctuated throughout my childhood. When I confessed that I had gone through his phone looking for clues about why their marital split had occurred—blaming him by default—he looked at me squarely and told me his story. "Here is how I've messed up, and here is how it takes two." This conversation saved our relationship. Eventually we got to a place where there was more to talk about than familial mess.

We all moved from Rego Park to Astoria—my mother and I in a ground-floor apartment off Broadway, my father in a fixer-upper off Astoria Boulevard. Living with my mother as I eyed independence was no easy task, so his home became my safe haven. There, we connected over a lot of things—music, especially. He kept three tall shelves filled with hundreds of CDs from celebrated establishments like Tower Records or Kim's Video and Music. He introduced me to experimental rock bands, folk singers, and jazz musicians. When he ran out of room on the shelf, he turned to the internet to satisfy his insatiable appetite. He drank wine, and I munched on snacks as we listened to Secret Machines' "Alone, Jealous and Stoned" or the striking instrumental "Your Hand in Mine" by Explosions in the Sky. He took me to an Ingrid Michaelson concert at Terminal 5. We genuinely enjoyed one another's company. As I entered adulthood, we were closer than we'd ever been.

"I think you've got something here, Rach."

We were sitting in his apartment when my father had just finished reading some minor press about the style blog I'd started as a high school senior. Initially it was only meant to be part of my college applications, but my inherent ambition and my geographical proximity to the fashion industry accelerated its popularity. In between college lectures, I attended fashion shows and published stories. I cut my teeth interning in fashion closets and marketing departments. (I'll never forget the quizzical looks on my supervisors' faces when designers or industry professionals recognized me as an equal in the room.)

The momentum excited me because I hadn't meant for the blog to take up so much space. I opened my eyes to the future. It stirred something in my father, too.

"I think you've got something, and you should see where it goes."

I knew what he was angling at. "You think I should leave— like actually drop out?" I asked. I'd recently transferred from one college to another and was hesitant to invite more disruption.

My father wasn't necessarily adventurous, and we certainly didn't have the financial cushion to justify it, but out of necessity he'd learned to take risks. "You can always go back," he said with a quick shrug.

I clicked my tongue in response. Time and time again, history proved there was no going back in this family. "Yeah, I know . . . but do you think I can actually do this?"

He paused, looking at his lap with the same stoic expression he assumed whenever making a big decision. "I want you to have more options than I did—I think this could be that," he finally replied. "There's room for you. Remember, the world is full of yes."

I moved into my father's spare room in Astoria. I hadn't lived with him since I was a teenager, but we fell into a rhythm. I relaunched my blog and called it a boutique content company. It was the definition of small but mighty. I worked around the clock. I scheduled meetings, liaised with contractors and partners, created content for the site, attended dinners and networking events. My father filled in operational gaps by organizing invoices and assisting in research for professional services. He was my shadow, cast off from visibility in a darkness of our own making.

We agreed that my father should assume a private role in the business for optics—because when he was done helping, he put on his suit and returned to his night shift at the gentleman's club. "Tell them I work in hospitality," he joked if anyone ever broached the subject of his "day job" to me.

Much of that time is now a blur. There were generational and professional divides. I relied on precisely two years of experience to navigate the nuances of the workplace. My father kept a filing cabinet in an age when everything was digitized. He dreamed of moving it into his future corner office. There was no method to our madness—just unrelenting hope that this was "going to work [out]." My father never defined how that endpoint should look, and I knew I didn't need to ask. I had a gut instinct that this chapter had an expiration date.

○ ◑ ●

Three years in, I had established some solid ground. In addition to the business's publishing arm and a newly launched consultancy, I had a small base of regular contributors I could call upon for certain projects. My father was still assisting with admin duties while working for the clubs at night. I had recently moved to Brooklyn to live with the man I'd eventually marry.

On a crisp September evening, my father and I made dinner plans at a beloved café in St. Marks Place. He had news he needed to tell me in person.

The country was on the cusp of a deafening, loud political season, and the energy in the city felt charged. I was glad to escape into the comfort of our familiar two-seat table. But I felt his eyes drift past me as we leaned against the restaurant's white brick wall.

"Should I be concerned?" I asked.

"No, no, nothing like that," he said with a soft chuckle. A few moments passed before he told me he was leaving New York. He was leaving to look after my grandmother and her sister in New Mexico. He was leaving because he was tired. "Besides, now that I know you're launched, I think it's time," he murmured. A few moments of silence passed, then a deep sob broke the tension. It was one of the few times in my life I'd

seen him cry. I took in my father's weathered face: Deep circles hung under his eyes; he pursed his lips as if trying to hold
back a twitch. The light outside was fading to dusk. While
I had run around the city trying to leave my mark, the city
marked my father in destructive ways. He kept certain things
about his other life close to the vest. It had only been a few
years since I'd gotten him back from the chaos of my youth—
but I knew I had to let him go.

His tears signaled a subtle change between us. "Sorry," he said
shakily. I nodded, trying to reestablish eye contact and holding back tears of my own.

In New Mexico, my father assumed the role of caretaker.
"You've been promoted to management now, Ma," he called
out whenever my grandmother came shuffling down the
driveway with an armful of gardening tools or branches
and weeds.

His new life oriented him toward a more traditional schedule,
away from his mind and back to his body. He rose early, tend-
ing to the expansive property, watering plants and clearing
debris, lining the pathways with gravel and fertilizer. He sent
photos of my grandmother's newest paintings. He recorded
his neighborhood walks, debriefing me on his errands while
I watched his sandaled feet kick up dirt from Corrales Road.
His skin browned and never burned. His big frame grew
stronger. He kept me close while, far away, I ran myself ragged.

Back at his desk, and Wi-Fi permitting, he'd update the business's QuickBooks account for me and correspond with what had blossomed into a global contributor roster. "Hiya, Rach!" he would text before sharing any updates that I needed to address. By that point, I found my heart sinking more than swelling when I received these messages. I had been secretly struggling to run things at full capacity, and now *I* was exhausted. A series of failed professional partnerships and missteps forced me to confront an issue I had turned away from for years: This wasn't sustainable. More to the point, I never exactly wanted to be a *founder*—when I started on this path, I was in the game of trying to find myself. Now, I felt like I had lost something instead. My sadness was eclipsed by the hope that flickered in my father's gaze. He believed in this—in me. Then one night, we turned the lights out and woke up to a new world.

In the absence of his physical presence, I began to see my father, which is to say, I began to see myself. I saw how our shared conscientiousness bordered on obsessiveness, how our anxieties about the future never waned, how our tendencies to withdraw were masked as "recharging," how we automatically assumed the worst-case scenario. It wasn't so much coming from a place of negativity as it was preventative: When the going got tough, my father and I knew to keep going—but we also knew to brace for impact. We had done it for so long already.

Working together was a means to a different end—we had something to build instead of clean up. We could be more productive versions of ourselves. We could be received well by others. We could hope for the best, because the world told us we were charting the best course forward. Our relationship with hope had become conditional—and the pandemic shook its definition to the very core. The world was no longer full of yes, but panic. It would be two years before we saw each other again.

As quarantine raged on, the days stretched out into sameness. Even in the stillness, I felt myself crossing a threshold. All sorts of changes were brewing.

Weeks into our new reality, I turned to the infamous filing cabinet I had taken when my father moved. In an effort to stay organized (and distracted), I transferred the once-packed drawers of paperwork onto a hard drive. Now, it mostly stored tangled cables and a pile of old diaries from my childhood. On a particularly bleak evening, I flipped through one of them, and in its pages, I came across a letter my father had sent me for my eighteenth birthday. A small portion of it reads:

"When I looked at your blog last night, I realized that you were going to be okay. . . . I am so proud of you, and I love you in a way that can't be described. Go out into the world now and take your place. Be full of the confidence you bring to all the things you do, and continue to be yourself. Fill your life with the people and things you love. Never settle for less. Choose your battles, and when you do battle, battle to win. When I see you later in time, I know people will be amazed at where you are and what you have done. I won't.

I'll just smile to myself and nod because I knew something they didn't."

○ ◐ ●

A father hides his exhaustion. A daughter hides her father. The world makes both of them want to hide from so much. Even when certain moments end and they leave something behind, the two of them never hide from one another.

My father left and kept leaving—initially for New Mexico and then Florida, where he lives now. Ultimately, he left the business, and almost immediately after, I tore it down abruptly and without ceremony. By then, life had irreparably changed, and I shed a skin—a name, a brand, a lifestyle, any expectations about what validated my worth. This chapter was over, but our most important work was just beginning.

He left to heal—to learn. He left and reminded me our closeness transcended borders or jobs. He left and showed me that even during our darkest moments, the world is full of yes, but it's also full of hope if we say yes to its questions.

I ask my father if he understands why I needed to let go of what we tried to build, and he tells me yes. I ask him if he's okay, and he tells me yes. I continue to ask him if *we'll* be okay, and he tells me yes, again and again and again. It's the story of our lives.

Now he mostly tells me about the weather and passing inter-actions with his neighbors. He lives alone and on his own terms for the first time in many years. He writes to me about his renewed sense of purpose and vigor: "I feel I can create another career for myself that will carry me well until I decide to retire and that I can establish control and dignity for the foreseeable future." His heart can finally roar louder than his voice. The only resonant sound is one of reawakening: a daughter finally finding herself and a father doing the same.

The darkness we inherit from our parents can be hard to reconcile; I have a habit of carrying it long and far. Only recently have I set it down and learned to look long enough to see the bright spot. I can see it—and say it—so clearly now: *When I looked at my father years later, I realized that he was going to be okay. I was so proud and loved him in a way that couldn't be described.*

My faith in my father is as strong as his faith is in me. I picture him riding his bike near the ocean, quietly nodding at the world that broke his heart and built it again. There he goes, finally living his life in the light.

Fill Your World with Yes

PROMPT

Try to imagine what you can say yes to in your life by keeping these daily prompts in mind.

MONDAY: What questions make you automatically respond with a yes? Write down as many questions as you can.

TUESDAY: What words or images immediately bring yes to mind? Write about why these things appeal to you or inspire action.

WEDNESDAY: When was the last time you automatically said yes to someone? Write about the circumstances and how it felt.

THURSDAY: When was the last time someone automatically said yes to you? Write about the circumstances and how it felt.

FRIDAY: What scares you about saying yes? Write about the opportunities or situations that you want to say yes to but that fill you with fear or uncertainty.

SATURDAY: What advice would you give to someone about saying yes? Write down what you would say—and then repeat it back to yourself word for word.

SUNDAY: Say yes to rest, and read the next story.

SLOW STORIES

On Potential

A big refrain in my life is one I've picked up from my father. "We'll see," he cautions whenever someone assumes something or asks about the future. While it may seem skeptical, it's also the perfect hidden invitation to slow down. To avoid becoming attached to definite outcomes. To see things precisely as they are. Despite the constant barrage of chaos, embracing slowness allows me to witness life moment by moment—and write it sentence by sentence. Sometimes, though, the words don't fit.

Writing this book allowed me to see potential in a new light: Ideas and phrases remained unripened even as I tried to put them on these pages. Questions and reflections bumped against my arguments or missed the point altogether. (The original book title even changed toward the end of the process.) But I couldn't abandon how certain things sounded and made me feel, even if those feelings pointed toward discomfort or sadness. They didn't belong in a graveyard, so I made a garden.

While it's the end of our time together, it's also the beginning of something else. Of what? I can't quite say. We'll just have to see. For now, I'll leave you with what remains—seeds instead of scraps or skeletons—because slow stories come alive in the most surprising places.

○ ◐ ●

A joke: What do you call a . . . ? Maybe you don't call them anything; you just give them a call. You ask them about the weather, and then they tell you about their world.

○ ◐ ●

After I recalibrate my pace—when *tension* is gradually replaced by *attention*—what happens next?

○ ◐ ●

At night, I whisper "sorry" out loud in the dark for a problem brewing deep inside.

○ ◐ ●

But the mess had some meaning: It was a kind of closeness that kept two people glued together when no one else could hold on.

○ ◐ ●

Crowded rooms alert me to what I lack and lose.

Dreams end. The best-case scenario is that you're the one doing the ending, but more often than we like, dreams morph into something less meaningful due to circumstance. Or they are taken away altogether. But that evolution shows us resilience, adaptability, and openness to growth. We grow every time we open our eyes.

Endings feel like a teardrop that finds a home above your cheekbone and under your eye. It lingers. When you've finally collected yourself, you can still feel its sticky remnants despite no longer being able to see it.

For now, we're together—part of a new chapter in our stories until the last sentence comes, and we're off again.

He left me in the dark about what he thought I needed so that I could turn my gaze toward the sun.

Just because the light is gone doesn't mean you can't see what you need to.

○ ◑ ●

I'm compelled to walk in wonder.

○ ◑ ●

I'm grateful to be able to point to so many places on the map and recall experiences. Now, though, the landscapes ooze into one another like watercolors.

○ ◑ ●

I hear a slightly annoying but melodic sound—something resembling the familiar, unpredictable soundtrack of family.

○ ◑ ●

I hope to keep him close with these words and the stories that begin long after these pages end.

○ ◑ ●

I like questions without great expectations—where there is room to breathe and stand by a one-word answer. To accept it. To move on and ask something else.

○ ◑ ●

I stopped listening to others, which is to say, I stopped trusting.

○ ◑ ●

I wander inside the recesses of my heart, looking for people and places who've become lost to time and circumstance.

If loss hardens us, perhaps leaving is a softer form of attention.

Loss of words means room for silence and, in it, a decision about how to pick up the pieces.

My family is good at fighting, but most of us have grown into people who don't refuse to know one another until it's too late. I think that's because we know ourselves best during profound loss.

Slowness narrows the path, but that way, it's easier to stay the course. There is less distraction or chance of getting hurt if we take our time. And if we do get hurt, we've moved in such a way that we greet healing as a series of small steps.

The other season likes to be recalled, not revered.

The shape of love is round.

○ ◑ ●

The sky wasn't falling—it was me. When I hit the ground,
I remembered to stand on it more firmly as I took the
next step.

○ ◑ ●

The things we want and the things we hope for don't always
look the same.

○ ◑ ●

There is a fine line between feeling grounded by memories
versus being weighed down by them.

○ ◑ ●

There is no easy way to begin a story about failures, but it's
even harder not to acknowledge that they happened.

○ ◑ ●

We spend so much time questioning how we got here and
what we'll do to move on, and in this way, time is passing.
Seasons are moving in and out of us like a hurricane.

○ ◑ ●

When hope is weaponized, everything shatters.

When I've followed my heart, it's led me to good people. It's now become a matter of trusting it again.

When people say, "You can't make this stuff up," I want to correct them because you *can*, in fact, make it up. We make up our lives every day—the trick is to make it all work in harmony.

Why do you willingly surrender to strangers but turn away from those you love?

You look for your people, and then you finally see them for who they are. Then life does what it does, and you learn to let things go.

Take It Piece by Piece

PROMPT

All we can do is take things day by day—or piece by piece.
Consider isolated moments or ideas, and write about how
they can inspire or fit into your slow story in new ways.

MONDAY: Go through an old notebook, diary, or
planner—physical or digital—and pull the first line
of text you see. Make that the first sentence of a
short story or letter.

TUESDAY: Reflect on a moment of anger or sadness.
What was said then, and how would you respond to
a past version of yourself today?

WEDNESDAY: Write about a one-line text, email, or message you received that unexpectedly inspired you. Was
it because of the tone, the content, or the sender?

THURSDAY: Listen to a piece of three of your favorite
songs. Write down the lyrics side by side and consider
how these phrases make you feel when they're all
together and when they're apart.

FRIDAY: Write about the unrelated pieces of your life
that form a pattern. Why do you think you're drawn to
specific aesthetic details or words?

SATURDAY: Revisit your favorite piece of art—a painting,
book, song, poem, or film—and ask yourself how this
work applies to your life or what meaning you can glean
from it today.

SUNDAY: Write the first thing that comes to mind—then
let it go. Rest and begin again.

Acknowledgments

Writing encompasses so much of what I value: creativity, quiet, solitude. But as a first-time author, I've learned just how special it is to invite feedback and collaboration into this process. Luckily, my support system stretches across the globe. Words can't describe how thrilled I am to have crossed paths with so many amazing people. Special thanks to

My agent, Kate Woodrow, for seeing me. I'm forever grateful for our partnership.

My editor, Rachel Hiles, for seeing this book. I couldn't have asked for a better collaborator and champion.

Everyone at Chronicle Books for bringing my words into the world with style and care.

Tyler and Emily Freidenrich for offering invaluable industry insight—and unmatched kindness.

Sanaë Lemoine for the early (and genuine) encouragement of this book.

Meredith Westgate and Ella Frances Sanders for nourishing
hours-long talks about writing, life—the deep stuff.

Kayla Maiuri for kindly advising on early drafts of
"Mountain Time" and "Remember the Good."

Fanny Singer, Evan Lian, Allison Strickland, Virginia
Sin, Sophia Roe, Caitlin Barasch, Nicholas Barasch,
Lyn Slater, Echo Hopkins, Teresa Hopkins, Nicole Loher,
Rachel Fleit, Leah Thomas, Jezz Chung, Liz Beecroft,
Anisa Benitez, Anna Hogeland, Olivia Joffrey, Ali LaBelle,
Anamaria Morris, Tonya Papanikolov, and Natalia Swarz
for your time and participation. I'm honored to include
your voices in these pages.

Pepper, for being a true angel from above, even though
you're round on the ground.

My grandmother for continually teaching me about
art, family, and humanity. (And for the care packages
of all kinds!)

My parents for their unending love and support.
For everything.

My husband, John McLaughlin, for standing by me
through it all. I love you forever.